Rediscovered

Challenging Centuries of Misinterpretation and Neglect

Ariel and D'vorah Berkowitz

Foreword by Dr. David Stern

First Fruits of Zion
PO Box 620099
Littleton, Colorado 80162-0099
E-mail: ffoz@net-mgmt.com

First edition July 1996
Second edition December 1996

Published in Israel

ISBN 965-90104-0-0

Distributed by

First Fruits of Zion, Inc.
PO Box 620099
Littleton, Colorado 80162-0099 USA
Phone: (303) 933-2119 or (800) 775-4807
Fax: (303) 933-0997 / E-mail: ffoz@net-mgmt.com

Dedication

This book is dedicated to all those in pursuit of Torah
and to the loving memory of our fathers
Edward Berkowitz ז״ל
and
Dr. Michael J. Vaccaro ז״ל
who taught us to embark on the pursuit of truth.

Contents

Acknowledgments

We owe a special debt of gratitude to Boaz Michael and his wife Tikvah, both for encouraging us to write this book and for their hours of sacrifice in physically producing it. We also want to thank Lev Kohen, Veronica McAlpine, Rittie Katz, Shoshanah Bat T'zion, Nirit Zagofsky, and others (you know who you are!) for their time and effort. And of course, *todah rabah* to Murray and Kay Silberling and Dov Chaikin for their constructive suggestions for the second edition of this book.

Had it not been for all of our companions in the pursuit of truth—those of you whom the Lord has led into our path as we served Him leading groups and congregations—this book could not have been written. You are the farmers, insurance brokers, housewives, businessmen, rabbis, college staff, and more. We met you in Templeville, Maryland; Penacook, New Hampshire; Boston and Worcester, Massachusetts; Tiberias, Jerusalem, and other parts of Israel. Thank you for the input you have given us which has helped to shape many of the concepts expressed in this book. All of you have been a challenging stimulus and a great encouragement to us.

And finally, we thank God for the four wonderful children He has given to us, Beth, Rachel, Becky and Joel. Through the many joys and challenges of raising them, God has always confirmed to us the plethora of practical truths in the Torah for their courageous pursuit of His truth.

Foreword

By David H. Stern

I count it a privilege to have Ariel and D'vorah Berkowitz as friends and neighbors here in Jerusalem. I consider it an honor to be asked to write the foreword for their book on Torah. I am pleased to see my name and books among the references quoted in the text. But most of all I think I can regard this book itself as in some degree a fruit of my own ministry in the Messianic Jewish movement.

In my book, *Messianic Jewish Manifesto*, which Ariel read soon after it appeared in 1988, I urged Messianic Jews to lead the Body of Messiah in reacquainting Christian theologians in particular and the Church at large with the centrality of Torah in the Gospel. The Berkowitzes now join the small but growing number of Messianic Jewish writers who are doing just that.

In this regard they go beyond the Christian scholars who are starting to appraise Paul's attitude toward the Torah more favorably than past generations of theologians; for these scholars, perhaps in the name of objectivity, usually approach the question much more abstractly, much more gingerly. Their work is appreciated, but at the same time we need people who will get down to brass tacks and talk about *how to live* by the Torah.

Ariel and D'vorah don't have all the answers; neither did I in my chapter on Torah in *Manifesto* (the longest chapter in the book). But they are addressing the right question and carrying the discussion a bit further than before. They are giving all of us food for thought. For the production of guidelines for behavior (known in Judaism as *halacha*, the "way to walk") necessarily must be a communal product, not decreed by scholars in ivory towers, but growing out of the life of a holy community trying, by the power of the Spirit of God, to live out what it means to be a new creation in Yeshua the Messiah.

Ariel's experience as a pastor in America and as a teacher here in Israel—and D'vorah's experience as a pastor's wife—along with their years of study, expressed in their own walk of faith, give them background and experience for writing this book. I am glad that they have decided to share that background and experience. May the reader come away with an enhanced understanding and appreciation for the role of the Torah in the Gospel and an increased desire to embrace it in the light of New Testament truth.

David H. Stern, Ph.D.
Translator, Jewish New Testament
Author, Jewish New Testament Commentary
Jerusalem, Israel

Prologue

Hilkiah's Discovery

It had been an unusually long day for Hilkiah the high priest. Under the direction of his godly king Josiah, he was busy supervising the repair work Josiah had ordered for the Temple in Jerusalem. Even though there were masons and carpenters everywhere, there were things which only he, the high priest, was able to do, places where only he was authorized to go. The Temple had not been repaired in years, and Hilkiah was working very hard.

We are not sure where it was, nor what time of day, but during one of his tedious work shifts Hilkiah found something that would revolutionize the nation. As he was removing some of the centuries-old debris and many of the Temple implements which had fallen into disuse, he came across an old scroll. Blowing off the dust, he could see that this was a rather important law document. But he needed the assistance of the scribe Shaphan in order to determine precisely what it said.

We can imagine the mixture of excitement and fear that must have gripped Shaphan as he began to read the ancient Hebrew letters. Making his way through the workmen, he headed straight to the palace: he had to speak directly to the king. After reciting a quick progress report on the Temple repairs, Shaphan could contain himself no longer. As if no one else were present, he announced to King Josiah, "Hilkiah the high priest has given me a book!" He then proceeded to read the scroll in its entirety.

Hilkiah knew this book was something special; so did Shaphan. No one, however, was as deeply moved as King Josiah. It did not take him long to realize that this scroll was none other than a copy of the Torah which Moshe had received from the Holy One. Upon hearing its words, Josiah did the only thing that was appropriate when the Word of God was read after so long a period of time: "And it came about when the king heard the words of the book of the Torah, that he tore his clothes." Then he commanded Hilkiah, Shaphan and the other spiritual leaders to "Inquire of the Lord for me and the people and all Judah concerning the words of this book that has been found, for great is the wrath of the Lord that burns against us, because our fathers have not listened to the words of this book, to do according to all that is written concerning us."

After King Josiah heard this rediscovered Torah, God so moved in his life that he immediately embarked upon a massive spiritual reform movement such as Judah had never seen. Idols and places of false worship were removed from both the Temple itself and all around Jerusalem and Judah. Moreover, we are told that Israel celebrated Passover in a manner not seen since the days of the judges! In the end, the Lord said of Josiah, "And before him there was no king like him who turned to the Lord with all his heart and with all his soul and with all his might, according to all the Torah of Moshe, nor did any like him arise after him." (All quotations from II Kings 22 and 23)

Hidden, but Not Lost

Even though Hilkiah's rediscovery of the Torah took place around the year 632 BCE, we can find in this historical account several significant parallels to life among the people of God today.

First, note that the Torah was not lost, but merely hidden among the ruins of the Temple of God. The same is true for us. The body of Messiah, according to the *Brit Hadasha* (New Covenant), is the temple of the living God. Yet for centuries, the Torah has for the most part remained hidden and misunderstood, its true nature and value unknown. Here and there, believers have seen glimpses of it, but by and large the Torah has lain ignored, collecting dust amid all the religious trappings held in high esteem by the people of God.

Beloved, the Spirit of God is causing more and more of God's people to "rediscover" His ancient words. No longer is the Torah just a children's storybook featuring our favorite Bible characters. Believers are rediscovering it as a book of the covenant given to God's redeemed people, as a document describing the lifestyle for the holy community, and as the sacred marriage agreement between God and His people. Indeed, today, more than 2,500 years since Hilkiah's monumental find, believers in all parts of the world are making the same rediscovery for their own personal and corporate lives.

Found in Judah

There is a second parallel. The Torah was first recovered among the people of Judah—and rightly so, as it was first and foremost a Jewish document, a covenant between God and the children of Israel. This is also the case today. In the past thirty years, more Jewish people have come to believe in Messiah Yeshua than perhaps in all the previous centuries except the first! That is quite a significant movement of God. And since the Lord is turning many of the children of Israel to Himself, it only makes sense that He is also opening the eyes of many Jewish believers to the privileges and responsibilities of the Torah.

Fortunately, God has not restricted this movement to the physical children of Israel. An increasing number of those who have been grafted in to Israel—the non-Jewish believers in Yeshua—are also beginning to understand the wonders of Torah.

Significant Spiritual Changes

One further element of Hilkiah's discovery bears mentioning. The rediscovery of the Torah led those who understood its full import to make immediate and significant changes in their lives. The natural leader in this, having been so deeply affected by the Torah himself, was King Josiah. We have already seen that this rediscovery of Torah culminated in a national Passover observance. It is significant to note that it also led to a greater appreciation of the doctrines of redemption!

For many years, the body of Messiah all over the world has been praying for revival. In some places these prayers are being answered. But especially in the western world, where the majority of Jewish people live, this long-anticipated revival has yet to transpire. Could it be that when believers begin to make Torah their guide for life, and to participate in the annual celebrations disclosed in it, they will see—as did the believers of ancient Israel—what redemption truly is? Whatever the case, all who are currently learning to apply the Torah to their lives are experiencing deep-seated and profound spiritual growth.

This Book: A *Shadchan*

We have chosen the account of Josiah and the rediscovery of the Torah as a prologue to this book because of the direct parallels between Josiah's time and ours. Just as he and his subjects embraced the words of the scroll unearthed so long ago, many individuals and fellowships today are beginning to rediscover the Torah for themselves, and are happily reaping the results of their findings.

The purpose of this book is to help you rediscover the Torah for yourself. These pages are intended to help you get to know the Torah as it truly is, the written Word of God. In other words, we want to function as a Jewish *shadchan*, a matchmaker who brings couples together in the hope that a wonderful and lasting marriage will result.

May we be your matchmaker, your shadchan? We want to introduce you to a wonderful, loving, giving, gracious and beneficent friend: the Torah. We want to help you get to know it, to see not only its beauty, but all of the other magnificent qualities it possesses.

Please ignore any rumors you may have heard. Give Torah a chance! King Solomon spoke about wisdom the way we would speak of Torah:

> Wisdom calls aloud in the street, she raises her voice in the public squares; at the head of the noisy streets she cries out, in the gateways of the city she makes her speech: Her ways are pleasant ways, and all her paths are peace. She is a tree of life to those who embrace her; those who lay hold of her will be blessed. By wisdom a house is built, and through understanding it is established; through knowledge its rooms are filled with rare and beautiful treasures. (Proverbs 1:20–21; 24:3–4 [NIV])

This book is intended to help those who have never had a chance to get to know Torah or to discover what a joy it can be. To be sure, it can be misused, but if related to in the way God designed, we are certain that Torah will give you many happy years together, ushering you into new depths of intimacy with your God.

This book was not designed to be an exhaustive theological treatise, although all that is written herein is based on solid biblical theology. Rather, we wrote it for those who are finding a new stirring coming from deep within their hearts to know the true Torah—both the written Word and the Word made flesh who dwells among us, Yeshua the Messiah. Our prayer is that this meeting will result in a match!

Introduction

If there is one area of misguided theological thinking for believers, it is the study of Torah. In fact, most evangelical Bible colleges and seminaries do not even have an area of study called "Torah." In contrast, however, the study of Torah is one of three main areas of study in *yeshivot* (Jewish religious training institutions) and Jewish seminaries, along with "God" and "The People of Israel." This means, according to Messianic Jewish scholar David Stern, that at least one third of the material studied by potential rabbis is hardly even considered by evangelical believers. Is it any wonder that, when the followers of Yeshua get together with Jewish people who do not yet know their Messiah, there is very little to talk about?

Stern crystallizes the need for believers to wake up to the necessity of understanding the Torah when he comments, "I believe that Christianity has gone far astray in its dealings with the subject and that the most urgent task of theology today is to get right its view of the law [Torah]."[1]

In this book, we will begin to delve into the rediscovering of Torah. First, we will examine the Torah as a document. In Chapter Two, we will look into its various purposes. Chapter Three will examine the Torah as a way of life. In Chapters Four and Five, we will see who may follow the Torah, and explore some of their motivations for doing so. Finally, the main body of the book will conclude with a brief discussion of Jewish and Christian misconceptions of the Torah.

What Are We Talking About? The Definition of Torah

In traditional Jewish thinking, the word "Torah" refers in a rather broad sense to all the authoritative teachings of the rabbis. But there are a number of other definitions in use as well:

- All Jewish law, as recorded in both the Bible and the Talmud (a compendium of oral Torah)

- The Tenach (the complete Old Testament)

- The first five books of the Bible, Genesis through Deuteronomy (also called the Chumash)

- The covenant God gave to Moshe (Moses) on Mount Sinai (because it contains individual teachings, or torahs)

- Any teaching of the first five books of the Bible

Rabbinic Jewish thinking has declared that there are two Torahs: written and oral. When the rabbis speak in these terms, they usually define the written Torah as the *Chumash* (Pentateuch, or first five books of the Bible). This Torah was written by Moshe as he received it from God Himself on Mount Sinai. On the other hand, the oral Torah, the rabbis claim, was also received by Moshe from God on Mount Sinai. However, this Torah was passed down through the centuries by word of mouth rather than the written word. Perhaps the clearest statement of this idea is found in *Pirke Avot* ("Sayings of the Fathers"), a section of the *Mishnah* (the written version of the oral Torah). In Avot 1:1 we read, "Moshe received Torah at Sinai and handed it on to Joshua, from Joshua to the elders, from the elders to the prophets, and the prophets handed it on to the men of the Great Assembly."

Eventually this oral material was itself written down, beginning around the year 200 CE under the authority of Rabbi Yehuda haNasi. It is worth noting that since the rabbis believe this material to have come from God at Mount Sinai, for them it carries almost as much authoritative weight as the written Chumash. For us it does not. By saying this, however, we do not mean that there is no value in reading and studying the Talmud and other rabbinic writings. A complete discussion of this subject can be found in Chapter Six of this book.

For our purposes here, we will use the word "Torah" in two ways: first, to refer to the first five books of the Bible—all of which, we assert, are from the mouth of God and written with perfect accuracy by the hand of Moshe—and second, in reference to the specific teachings within the Five Books of Moshe.

Let us begin by reintroducing this divine document to you. You may have known it previously as a list of do's and don'ts. Now it is time for you to examine the unique and diversified document God's Torah truly is!

Chapter One
A Unique Document

A Unique Document

Having defined what we mean by "Torah," let us now look at what kind of document it is. To some this may seem like a superfluous question. "It is law," they say. True, it does contain some laws. But upon more careful examination, we discover that Torah is far beyond this rather simplistic description.

Teaching

First and foremost, the Torah is God's teaching. This is the primary meaning of the Hebrew word *Torah* (תורה). The word does not mean "law"; it means "teaching." Moreover, the root for "Torah" can be traced to the Hebrew word meaning "to shoot an arrow," or "to hit the mark." Thus, "The word 'Torah' means literally, 'teaching,' whether it is the wise man instructing his son, or God instructing Israel."[2] Hence, we can say that "Torah" is God's teaching, hitting the mark of man's needs, including his need to know who God is and what His righteousness looks like.

Torah is a document in which God has revealed Himself to mankind and taught us about Himself and His righteousness. In the Torah, one can learn all the theological concepts which are expanded upon throughout the rest of the Bible, such as sin, sacrifice, salvation, sanctification—and Messiah, the One who accomplishes it all.

A Covenant

Second, Torah is a covenant. By this we mean that Torah is a legally binding agreement between God and His own people. The evidence for this is overwhelming. The Torah refers to itself several times as a covenant (*brit*). Any number of references could be cited, but two should be sufficient.

The first passage is Exodus 34:27. The context is the giving of the first written revelation, which included the Ten Commandments as well as other instruction. "And the Lord said to Moshe: 'Write down these commandments, for in accordance with these commandments I make a covenant [brit] with you and with Israel.'"

The second reference is Deuteronomy 29:1. Moshe is nearing the end of his life, over 40 years after the events in Exodus 34. He has recorded much more of God's teaching and instruction. Now, soon to enter the Promised Land, Moshe summarizes all the teaching from God and calls it, again, a covenant. He says:

> These are the terms of the covenant which the Lord
> commanded Moshe to make with the Israelites in
> the land of Moab, in addition to the covenant which
> He had made with them at Horeb.

Since Torah is a covenant, both parties involved are subject to certain legal obligations. God, the One who initiated this covenant, legally binds Himself to keep His word which He spoke in the covenant. Israel, the recipient of this agreement, is likewise bound to do the same. In a sense one could say that, understood in this light, Torah is really the national constitution for the nation of Israel. This becomes especially clear when, in the light of historical research, Torah is examined as a covenant and compared to other national covenants of its time.

There has been much documentation in recent years for the fascinating research accomplished by scholars like George Mendenhall, Meredith Kline and others. They have compared the documents of Torah with other documents in the same historical time frame (the fifteenth through thirteenth centuries BCE). Specifically, written treaties between nations and their conquered or vassal nations have been examined and compared with Torah. The similarities in form and structure are striking. These parallels are extremely helpful in further enhancing our understanding of Torah as a covenant document.

To illustrate this, let us compare the typical form of an ancient Hittite treaty with the format of the book of Deuteronomy. It has been found that the standard outline for such vassal treaties approximates the following:

Preamble—a basic introductory paragraph of the covenant

Historical Prologue—the acts of the great king, what he has done for the vassal nation

Stipulations—the main bulk of the treaty/covenant, the expectations of the vassal nation

Blessings and Curses—rewards for compliance and penalties of noncompliance with the covenant

Witnesses—the signatures of certain prominent figures who are party to the enactment of the covenant

Means of Succession (optional)—provision in the covenant for determining who will take the place of the great king

Provision for Depositing the Covenant (optional)—discusses where the covenant or copies of the covenant will be stored

Now let us compare this format with Deuteronomy:

Preamble (Deuteronomy 1:1–5)—gives basic introductory remarks about the book of Deuteronomy

Historical Prologue (Deuteronomy 1:6–4:49)—a recounting of what the Great King (God) has done for Israel

Stipulations (Deuteronomy 5:1–26:19)—the bulk of the book, known to laymen as "law"; more accurately, the stipulations given by God, the Great King, to Israel for the maintenance of this covenant

Blessings and Curses (Deuteronomy 27–30)—the consequences for Israel of keeping or breaking the covenant

Witnesses (Deuteronomy 30:19)—God calls upon heaven and earth to witness this covenant

Succession (Deuteronomy 31:1–8)—God provides for Joshua to follow Moshe when he dies

Deposit/Reading (Deuteronomy 31:9–13)—provision made to store the covenant in the ark and to read it publicly at a certain time

What does all this tell us? For one thing, from a historical perspective, the clear parallels between these vassal treaties and the Torah serve to buttress the evangelical contention that the Torah is what it presents itself to be—a coherent document written by Moshe in the middle to late second millennium BCE.

Second, we can now begin to see that the Torah is not just a list of do's and don'ts. It is, rather, a critically important document describing the legally binding relationship between God and Israel. Furthermore, it was given by God to serve as the national constitution for the nation of Israel. For in it we have everything from a preamble (comparable to a "We the people" in the US Constitution) to a verification by formal witnesses. The "do's and don'ts" are merely the legal requirements by which Israel, the redeemed nation, can maintain its covenant relationship before the Great King and enjoy the benefits thereof.

A *Ketubah*

Although Torah describes itself as a legal covenant, and we have seen that it functions as a national constitution as well, there is a portion within the Torah which hints at its being still another kind of document. One cannot be too dogmatic on this point, but there seems to be considerable evidence within the Torah which would prompt one to label it a *ketubah*. A ketubah is a formal written document which spells out the terms of a Jewish marriage contract. "The 'ketubah' also has a symbolic meaning. Since the bride and the groom represent Israel and God at Sinai, when the Torah was given, the ketubah represents the 'book of covenant' "—the Torah![3] Thus, according to Rabbi Kaplan, there is a connection between the Torah and the marriage contract.

The first hint of this is found in Exodus 6:6–7. In this passage, God tells Moshe what He intends to do for Israel through him. In short, God says that He will "set them apart"; He will "deliver" them from their bondage (bring them out from under the yoke of slavery); He will "redeem" them; and He will "take" them to be His people. (Those of you familiar with *Pesach* [Passover] will remember that these four verbs become names for each of the four cups of wine taken during the *Seder* [Passover meal]).

The last verb, "will take," is used elsewhere in the Tenach—among other uses, to describe what happens when a man "takes" a woman to be his wife. In the context of Exodus 6, then, it appears that God is betrothing Israel to be His wife. But when is the wedding?

According to traditional Jewish thinking, the wedding between God and Israel took place at Mount Sinai. Although the biblical text does not specify that a wedding was taking place, the similarities between the phenomena which occurred at Mount Sinai and a traditional Jewish wedding are striking. First, there was a *chuppah*, or canopy. We can see this in Exodus 19:9 when God says, "I will come to you in a thick cloud...." The cloud was a covering which can be seen to symbolize the chuppah under which the bride meets the Groom.

Every groom has an endearing name for his bride which reminds him of how much she means to him. God gave Israel such a name. In Exodus 19:5–7, God tells Israel that she is His "treasured possession." The Hebrew word, *segulah*, is also found in secular texts from this same period. It was used by kings to describe how precious they considered certain objects from a conquered nation. While the king valued all of his possessions, only a certain few treasures were especially cared for, protected, and honored. These were his *segulot*. Thus, when God calls Israel His segulah, it is a most endearing term. He cares for all His creation, but He considers Israel His special bride.

One of the main ingredients of the wedding is the ketubah itself—which, in addition to proving the legality of the marriage, serves to remind both parties of their mutual responsibility in making that marriage work. In this case, the ketubah is Torah as summarized in Exodus 20: the marriage agreement between God and Israel. God even provided two copies, one for Himself and one for them! Both were to be kept in the ark. Thus, we read in Exodus 31:18, "When He finished speaking with him on Mount Sinai, He gave Moshe the two tablets of the pact [covenant], stone tablets inscribed with the finger of God."

Finally, what is a wedding without a ring? The ring serves as an outward symbol of the marriage covenant. Where is the ring in this marriage? It is found in Exodus 31:12–17. In verse 13, we are told that God gave the *Shabbat* (Sabbath) as a sign—in Hebrew, *ot* (אות)—between Himself and the children of Israel throughout the ages. In fact, so important is Shabbat as a sign of the covenant that it is repeated once more in this passage (verse 17). Hence, Shabbat is the ring, the outward sign of this marriage covenant.

Yeshua's Stamp of Approval

The Torah is unique because it is a covenant, a national constitution, and a marriage agreement. But it is also unique because of the way Yeshua related to it. Although not acknowledged as such in many circles today, our Messiah was the greatest Torah teacher who ever lived. And throughout His teachings runs the underlying assumption that God's covenant people are to have a living, meaningful, and ongoing relationship to Torah. In other words, in Yeshua's thinking, one of the Torah's main purposes is to describe the lifestyle of the redeemed community.

Matthew 5:17–20 teaches this very clearly. In this passage, Yeshua forthrightly states that He did not come to do away with the Torah. In addition, He rebukes all who attempt to invalidate it. He said, "Whosoever then annuls one of the least of these commandments, and so teaches others, shall be called least in the kingdom of heaven; but whoever keeps and teaches them, he shall be called great in the kingdom of heaven."

To back up His statement, He then embarks upon a series of teachings (Matthew 5–7) in which He challenges the popular understanding of several Torah passages by introducing

His own interpretations. He accomplishes this through the repeated use of the formula, "You have heard that the ancients were told [erroneous teaching of the rabbis], but I say unto you [correct interpretation]." This illumination of God's Word is what He was referring to when He said, "Do not think that I came to abolish the Torah or the prophets; I did not come to abolish, but to make the meaning full." (Matthew 5:17) Yeshua was speaking the common parlance of the rabbis of His day. According to scholars David Bivin and Roy Blizzard, Jr.,

> "Destroy" [abolish] and "fulfill" are technical terms of rabbinic augmentation. When a rabbi felt that a colleague had misinterpreted a passage of Scripture, he would say, "You are destroying the law!" What was "destroying the law" for one rabbi, was "fulfilling the law" (correctly interpreting Scripture) for another.[4]

If, as some say, the believer is to have no meaningful relationship to Torah, then this passage in Matthew would have been a most appropriate place for Yeshua to teach it. Clearly, He did not.

There is another important passage from the *Brit Chadasha* (New Covenant) which gives Yeshua's stamp of approval for the Torah. In Luke 24, following His resurrection, Yeshua revealed Himself to two of His followers while walking with them on the road to Emmaus. "Beginning with Moshe and with all the prophets, He explained to them the things concerning Himself in all the Scriptures." Again, in verse 44, He says something similar: "These are My words which I spoke to you while I was still with you, that all things which are written about Me in the Torah of Moshe and the Prophets and the Psalms must be fulfilled." Could it be that by using the word "fulfilled" He was saying that in order for Torah—and the rest of the *Tenach* (an acronym for the Old Testament)—

to be interpreted properly, one must see how it speaks of Himself?

Yeshua was saying, emphatically, that the Torah must be understood in such a way as to see Him in all of its teachings. This, by the way, establishes a critically important hermeneutical principle for proper interpretation of the Torah: we can learn how to follow any given teaching once we learn how it reveals the Messiah.

Furthermore, Yeshua's life was one of perfectly living out the written Torah. His teaching perfectly clarified and explained the Torah. He was so related to the Torah that some of His earliest followers referred to Him as *haTorah*—"The Torah"![5]

The Torah, then, is far more than a grand list of laws that are impossible to keep. It is an instructional document, teaching about God and His ways; a legal covenant between God and Israel; the national constitution of Israel, describing how the Great King Himself wants His nation to function within His kingdom; and a sacred marriage covenant between God (the Groom) and Israel (His bride).

However, while its role as a legal covenant is extremely important, the Torah was designed to fulfill many other functions as well. Let us look at some of these as we prepare to discuss how we can relate properly to the Torah as a whole.

Chapter Two
The Torah Can Do That?

The Torah Can Do That?

The Purposes of Torah

In Chapter One, we defined the Torah as a threefold document: first, a covenant between God and Israel; second, the national constitution of Israel; and third, the wedding ketubah between God, the Husband, and Israel, His bride. Based on these points, we can see several different purposes for the Torah, most of which are taught in the Brit Chadasha.

Sha'ul of Tarsus (Paul) was more than qualified to teach on the purposes of Torah because of his extensive rabbinic training and thinking. In many of his letters to various congregations of believers, he set forth the purposes of Torah—both negative and positive. Before we begin listing these, however, a word must be said regarding how to interpret Sha'ul properly. The reason for this is obvious. He, perhaps more than any other theologian, has been sorely misunder-stood and maligned by both Jewish and evangelical Christian scholars.

How to Understand Rav Sha'ul

One must bear in mind two basic hermeneutical principles when seeking to understand Rav Sha'ul. The first is the con-cept of keeping the harmony of the Scriptures intact. In other words, Scripture cannot contradict Scripture. For example, the events in Acts 21 occurred after Sha'ul had written both Galatians and Romans. In Acts 21, Sha'ul is clearly portrayed as a rather staunch follower of the Torah of Moshe, as were the tens of thousands of other Jewish believers in Yeshua! Please note particularly verses 15–26. Someone with the lead-ership status of Sha'ul of Tarsus would not live in a manner contrary to his teachings; that is, he would not have lived according to Torah while teaching other believers that it had no place in their lives. This would have rendered Sha'ul a hopelessly contradictory teacher, causing the Scriptures to be contradictory as well.

The second hermeneutical principle is *context*. Both the immediate context and that of the whole book or letter are important. Let us take Sha'ul's letter to the Galatians as an example. It is essential to know that the context for Galatians concerns people who believed that salvation was dependent upon obedience to the Torah. Because of this heresy, it stands to reason that Sha'ul's letter would contain many rather nega-tive statements concerning such a use of Torah. But such state-ments should all be interpreted in light of the context of the letter. Sha'ul's primary purpose in Galatians was not to teach on the application of Torah to the life of the believer, but rather to emphasize that one may not live according to Torah in order to earn, merit, or keep one's justification. The same idea would also apply to Romans.

Unfortunately, many interpreters of Sha'ul's writings have not applied these hermeneutical principles in a consistent fashion. Therefore, Sha'ul is portrayed either as mixed up, contradictory, anti-Jewish, or the founder of a new religion called "Christianity." He is none of the above! He is merely the kind of Jewish person God intended the sons of Jacob to be all along, faithfully engaged in bringing the Good News of the Messiah's atoning death and resurrection to the Gentiles and properly applying the message to them.

Now, with all this in mind, let us begin to outline some of Sha'ul's understanding of the purposes of Torah:

1. Torah is not to be observed in order to gain justification before God.

As stated above, this is the whole point of the letter to the Galatians, and one of the major points of the letter to the Romans. Romans 3:20 teaches, "By the works of the Torah [or any legal system, according to the context of Romans 2–3], no flesh will be justified in His sight." People were trying to observe the Torah (as well as other legal systems) in order to be saved. To such people Sha'ul emphatically said, "The Torah is useless!" Why useless? Because Torah is meant to be the lifestyle for someone who is *already* justified and redeemed.

2. Torah helps man to recognize his own sinfulness.

There are several statements in this regard throughout Sha'ul's epistles. The rest of Romans 3:20 will suffice to illustrate this. Sha'ul says, "for through the Torah comes the knowledge of sin." The Greek word translated "knowledge" should be rendered "recognition." Torah does not tell people what sin is; rather, it is through Torah that people can see the *sinfulness* of their sin! (This function of the Torah primarily concerns those who are not yet redeemed.)

3.   Torah helps to bring about God's wrath.

Romans 4:15 says, "For the Torah brings about wrath...."
Once again, knowing the context of this verse is extremely
important. Sha'ul's teaching in Romans stresses that if anyone tries to use Torah to achieve justification before God, the
attempt will backfire! He will only discover that he cannot
obey it perfectly, thus achieving only condemnation. Justification has always been and always will be granted as a gift
from God, on the basis of one's personal trust in that which
Yeshua accomplished through His atoning death and subsequent resurrection. If any person attempts to earn justification by trying to obey the Torah, then for him the Torah will
serve only to condemn. It was not designed for such a purpose.

4.   The Torah acts as a protector.

In Galatians 3:23ff, Sha'ul speaks of the Torah's role as a
protector. This idea requires a bit of explanation. First, let us
see what Sha'ul had in mind in Galatians, and then expand
more fully on the concept. We will conclude this section with
a simple summary.

The Pedagogue

Sha'ul was drawing upon a very familiar illustration from
the ancient Greco-Roman world of which he was a part. Well-
to-do families often hired someone to serve as a protector for
their children when they sent them to their teachers. The protector was not the teacher, but merely someone who made
sure that a child would safely reach his or her teacher. Sha'ul
uses this kind of language in Galatians 3:22ff to illustrate
how the Torah functioned as a protector.

How does God preserve such people? One way He has
chosen to do so, though certainly not the only way, is through
the Torah. According to Galatians 3:22ff, the Torah can func-

tion as a *pedagogue*, as the Greek word for "tutor" should be translated (verse 24). This pedagogue's duty was "to conduct the boy or youth to and from school and to superintend his conduct...he was not a 'teacher.'"[6] (Please note that the definition of the Greek word *paidagogos* differs from the modern English usage of "pedagogue.") Hence, he was something of a bodyguard to help ensure the student's safety on the way to his teacher.

In verse 23, Sha'ul explains this protective concept with a slightly different image. There he uses a word which has usually been translated as "kept in custody." However, by rendering the Greek verb *sugkleio* in such a manner, translators have unwittingly cast a negative shadow on the Torah, depicting it as something that holds people captive, like prisoners. But the word can have a slightly different connotation. It can also be rendered "close up," "hem in," or "enclose" in a positive sense. Seen in this light, the verse emphasizes protection rather than imprisonment. Furthermore, this translation also fits well with the concept of the pedagogue.

Thus, the Torah was intended to preserve the mental, moral and social safety of the environment into which an individual was born and raised. The person was protected "until the date set by the Father" (Galatians 4:2) when the Spirit of God would lead them to the Teacher, the Messiah. Let us now examine exactly how the Torah accomplishes this.

The "Law" Words

In order to get a grip on this function, we need to elaborate on our original definition of Torah. We have already established the fact that the word *torah* means teaching, or instruction. There are many such torahs in the collection of teachings we refer to as *the* Torah, the first five books of the Bible. And aside from the teachings themselves, the Torah also contains stories, poems, and historical writings (which are also teachings).

In addition, we find in the Torah another type of content very closely related to the word *torah*. We are referring to the *mishpatim*, *mitzvot*, and *chukim*. The most common way these words have been rendered into English is "judgments," "commandments," and "ordinances," respectively. These words emphasize the legal aspect of the Torah. In a sense, because of these words, the Torah is a "law." But it is not a law to be obeyed in order to secure or earn God's righteousness. Rather, it is a law which functions as a protective barrier. The judgments, commandments and ordinances, along with the teachings, all serve to protect God's people. It is very similar to the idea that we should "put a hedge around the Torah" (Pirke Avot 1:1). In this case, the rabbi is talking about other laws which should be used in order to protect the Torah from being broken. But the principle is the same. God's Torah, through its judgments, commandments, ordinances and teachings, is designed to put a hedge around people to protect them.

This hedge of protection operates in two ways. First, for the children on the way to the Teacher; and second, for God's holy community of the redeemed. As far as the children on the way to the Teacher—those to whom Sha'ul refers in Galatians 3:22ff—are concerned, the Torah can help preserve or protect their physical lives, keeping them safe until the Father calls them to believe in His Son. It does this by providing a safe environment in which they may live. The mishpatim, mitzvot, chukim, and other teachings of the Torah all help to create a safe community, surrounded by the protective border of the Torah. Anyone who lives within the confines of that border will live in relative safety. This does not mean that the person living within the borders of the Torah is automatically safe *spiritually*, or "saved"; rather, living within the Torah community, his life is being preserved and protected as he awaits the time set by the Father, his moment of salvation.

Take Leviticus 11 and the kosher foods as an example. The Torah states specifically that the purpose of the kosher foods was to set Israel apart from the idolatrous nations as a holy community. That very condition of being set apart from the corruption of the idolatrous nations around them puts them in a protected state, preserved by the teachings of Torah as they await the moment of salvation set by the Father in eternity past. The use of the words *mishpatim* and *chukim* in the reiteration of the kosher instructions in Deuteronomy 12 underscores the fact that these are "laws" serving to help protect. Therefore, the dietary teachings were designed by God to serve as a protector for His people from the corruption that surrounded them.

There is another sense in which the Torah can function for those who do not yet know the Messiah. What does the teacher look like to the person being led by the pedagogue? What are the characteristics of the Teacher's life and world?

Anyone living under the benefit of a holy community which follows the Torah will receive a more complete description of the Teacher. His mind will be preserved from inaccuracies and false images of what the Teacher looks like. He will be given accurate information and revelation of the Teacher, the Messiah.

Furthermore, the person on the way to the Teacher will be given a more accurate description of what life is with the Teacher. He will know what he is missing until that life becomes his, until he ceases to be merely "under the benefits" of the holy community and becomes an integral member of that community by sharing in the life of the Teacher, the Messiah Himself!

Protection for the Redeemed

If the Torah helps protect the lives of those not yet part of the redeemed community, how much more is it a safeguard for God's holy ones, those who believe? The mishpatim, mitzvot, chukim, and torot function as a protective border for the people of God.

This is illustrated in the diagrams on page 29. For our purposes, the pictures represent what are generally accepted as the original, God-intended borders of the theocracy of ancient Israel, functioning as a light to the nations around her (Deuteronomy 4:5–8). The pictures also depict the two spiritual realities of the universe: the kingdom of light (God's kingdom) and the kingdom of darkness (Satan's kingdom). Close study of Romans 5:12–21 will reveal the details of these two kingdoms.

The ruling power of the kingdom of light is life. The ruling power of the kingdom of darkness is death. It is important to remember that these two kingdoms exist whether man acknowledges them or not. They are part of the fundamental spiritual realities of the universe! If such an important reality as the kingdom of darkness exists, it is critical that we know where the boundaries of such a kingdom are located, in order that we might avoid participating in that kingdom. By the kindness, grace, and mercy of God, He has described for us exactly where the boundaries between these two opposite and diametrically opposed kingdoms lie. They are identified for us in the Torah (as well as its divinely inspired commentary, the Brit Chadasha). Moreover, the Torah is itself a boundary.

Let us take this two-kingdom concept one step further. That which is not of the kingdom of light and life is death, and therefore "unclean" for us—in other words, what we must not "touch" nor "eat of." These pictorial concepts teach us not to partake of nor participate in death (the kingdom of darkness). Such activities can only bring the fruit of death into our lives.

Because the Torah tells us the truth—the difference between holy and unholy, clean and unclean, life and death—it is both a protection for us and a written revelation of the grace of God. Every man, woman or child who chooses not to live within the teachings of God, which produce life, is consigned to a place outside of the blessing and protection established by these teachings. (Remember Deuteronomy 30:19–20.)

With this in mind, we can now begin to understand some of the more seemingly peculiar teachings of Torah, especially the so-called "legal" sections having to do with the theocracy of the kingdom of light. We can also tie in the description of the Torah as the national covenant and constitution, in which the Great King promises to protect His subjects through the covenant (see Chapter One). To protect them from what? From the kingdom outside of His kingdom: the kingdom of darkness. Remember that the chief characteristic of the kingdom of darkness is death, with all of its legal rights. The legal aspects of the Torah declare the truth that the kingdom of darkness has no jurisdiction inside the boundaries of God's kingdom—the Torah community.

The legal terminology of the Torah which, in many circles, gives rise to the belief that the Torah is "law" instead of a revelation of God's grace, can now be more clearly understood. These commandments make no sense unless we view them as living Torah teaching pictures, designed both to remind us of the realities of the two kingdoms and to keep us from participating in the kingdom of darkness.

Look, now, at the two diagrams (page 29). In Figure 1, we see a picture of the kingdom of light in the shape of the ancient theocracy of Israel. It is bordered by the actual words of the Torah. Outside those borders is the kingdom of darkness. *Please note that this diagram is not meant to imply that the nations outside of Israel are the kingdom of darkness!* It is simply an illustration of the Torah's intended function as a protector. If we remain within the borders established by the teachings of Torah, we will enjoy our God-given inheritance and be protected from the influences of the idolatrous peoples around us. We will also serve as a light to those nations.

This is also the reason behind the commands of Torah regarding those living in Israel who violate the Torah and must be put out of the community. One of the purposes of Israel was to be a place of safety, blessing and teaching. When a person violated this sacred place, he had to be removed from it for the sake of the rest of the holy community, until he either repented or was judged by God. Furthermore, this is also the reason that the "alien"—the non-Jewish person living among the inhabitants of the Holy Land—must live according to the Torah. For the sake of all those called to live in the Land, no act of rebellion can be allowed to compromise its holiness.

In Figure 2, we see that the teachings of the Torah establish "the place" (*haMakom*, המקום) where believers can partake of and enjoy the blessings that the teachings establish. The statutes that God laid down for us "are sweeter than honey and the honeycomb, and righteous altogether. By them your servant is warned, and in keeping them there is great reward." (Psalm 19:10–11)

The written Torah cannot and does not impart life (Galatians 3:21). The Torah community, created by obedience to the Torah, is the place where life reigns instead of death. It is the place of safety and teaching. "The statutes You have laid down are righteous, they are fully trustworthy" (Psalm 119:38) to "close up, hem in, and close within a place" (Galatians 3:23). What place? HaMakom, the place of blessing! By so doing, then, the Torah "hits the mark" of defining wherein lies the place of blessing and life.

To Enjoy the Blessings

There is another sense in which Torah acts as the protector of the redeemed community: it helps the community to enjoy

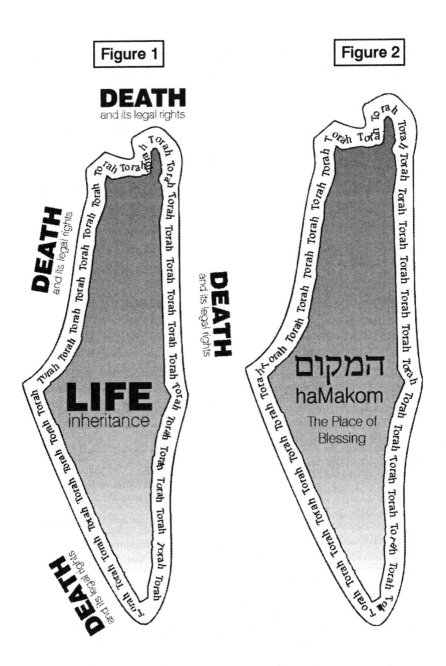

Figure 1

DEATH and its legal rights

DEATH and its legal rights

DEATH and its legal rights

DEATH and its legal rights

LIFE inheritance

Figure 2

המקום
haMakom

The Place of Blessing

Torah = the teaching of God that "hits the mark"

the benefits of their inheritance. To understand this concept, we need to examine how Sha'ul compares the two covenants— the one God made with Abraham in Genesis 12, and the one He made with Moshe in Exodus 19ff (often called the Torah)—in Galatians 3:10–21.

Sha'ul describes the covenant with Abraham as one in which God promises an inheritance to His people, which is intended to be received by faith. Notice the three elements: promise, inheritance, and faith. The promise of an inheritance was given by the grace of God, and the expected covenant response was faith. This is clearly taught in Genesis 15. Here God promises the inheritance which Abraham was to receive by faith.

In regard to the covenant with Moshe (Torah), Sha'ul first says in verse 12 that this is not a faith covenant. In other words, the expected covenant response was not faith, but obedience. Second, it was not a covenant of promise. It did not promise the inheritance, but merely protected the already redeemed people to enjoy and participate in the blessings of the inheritance! Moreover, verse 17 specifically states that the covenant with Moshe did not do away with the covenant with Abraham. Instead, the two complement each other.

Thomas McComiskey comments on the masterful interaction between these two covenants in his book, *The Covenants of Promise*:

> Not only did the law covenant define and amplify the promise, but it served to protect and secure the promise as well....The protective function of the law is also apparent in the various legal stipulations. The health laws and the prohibitions against Canaanite practices served to preserve the nation and to maintain its solidarity....The law also served to define the terms of obedience for those whose faith

was in the promise it perpetuated....The law is not the promise; it is a covenant distinct from the promise covenant. It establishes the conditions under which the terms of the promise could be maintained....The law did not give the inheritance; it served to provide the framework necessary for the people to maintain their relationship to it.

Hence, according to McComiskey, people were not saved by obeying the Torah, but by trusting in the promises of God. To participate in that eternal inheritance requires faith. But the Torah was given to the redeemed community, not an unsaved one (although there were unsaved people dwelling among the redeemed community), in order that the community could be maintained and protected. Obedience, therefore, is the required covenant response. Is this not what is taught in Galatians 3?

Looking at Torah in this context will help us to see its purposes and limitations more clearly. The following chart will help summarize what we have been saying about the purpose of the Torah, especially as it is compared to the covenant with Abraham:

Covenant with Abraham	Covenant with Moshe
Nature of the Covenant **Promise**	Nature of the Covenant **Blessing, maintenance, and enjoyment of promises**
Covenant response **Faith**	Covenant response **Obedience**

Let us clarify something here. In ancient Israel there were, in reality, two different kinds of people living in the same community. First and foremost were those who were not only physically redeemed from slavery in Egypt, but also redeemed from slavery to sin. These were the "remnant" which has existed throughout all of Israel's history down to this present age. This group, of unspecified number, were real believers who trusted in the Lord and His provision of atonement. For them, obedience to the Torah came *out of* or *because of* their faith. Their obedience did not earn them redemption, nor did it secure their relationship with God. It was simply a natural result of their faith, as we see in James 2:18.

The second group, again of undetermined size, were part of the redeemed community by virtue of the fact that they lived among the others and were required to follow the laws of the community. These people were not partakers of the covenant with Abraham, nor of the covenant with Moshe. Although physically redeemed from slavery in Egypt, they did not trust in God for their righteousness. They adhered to some of the statutes of the Mosaic covenant, perhaps even bringing the required sacrifices; however, this was not evidence of faith and trust in God, but a show of compliance intended to secure the protection of living in the holy community.

A person cannot appropriate the full blessings of the covenant with Moshe (the Torah) unless he first enters into the covenant with Abraham. The latter is done by faith and faith alone. The covenant of promise (through Abraham) gave Israel the physical promises. Not only are these physical promises a reality; they are also pictures of the spiritual relationship we have with God. Moreover, they are illustrative of the spiritual promises of inheritance obtained by all believers through faith in Yeshua.

For those who trust God for the promises, the proper order for faith and obedience is set by the sequence in which the covenants were given. In other words, faith must precede obedience. But the kind of faith accepted by God is one which naturally flows into obedience. True obedience never comes before faith, nor is it an addition to faith. It is always the *result* of true biblical faith. To rephrase this in terms of the covenants, the covenant of promise (Abraham) must come before the covenant of obedience (Moshe). If we were to put Moshe first, attempting to secure those promises by obedience, we would be going against God's order. (This, by the way, is the key to unlocking the difficult *midrash* used by Sha'ul in Galatians 4:21–31.) All we could hope for would be a measure of physical protection and a knowledge of spiritual things. But we could not receive justification nor a personal relationship with the Holy One through obedience to the Torah; it all had to start with faith. Abraham came before Moshe, but Moshe did not cancel out Abraham! The two complemented each other—as long as they came in the proper order.

At this point, let us summarize what we have said about the protective nature of the Torah. The Torah serves as a protector on three levels. First, if obeyed, it protects the nation to enjoy its inheritance. Second, it protects the individual redeemed people within that nation to enjoy their own inheritance. They truly enjoy to the fullest their redemption because they understand and participate in the miracle of redemption as portrayed by the mitzvot of Torah. And third, the Torah protects those who do not yet know the Teacher (Messiah) until the time God chooses to reveal Himself to them.

Chapter Three
The Torah—A Way of Life

The Torah—A Way of Life

As we have already seen, the Torah is not for those who are yet unregenerate; the only functions it serves for them is to point out their sin and subsequently to condemn them for it. However, the Bible does teach that the Torah is to be the way of life for the redeemed community. Deuteronomy 30:14–15 comments on the Torah by saying, "But the word is very near you, in your mouth, and in your heart, that you may observe it. See, I have set before you today life and prosperity." Jeremiah 31:33 again emphasizes that for the believer, "I shall put My Torah within them, and on their heart I will write it." Psalm 119 is completely dedicated to the blessings of living according to the Torah.

The Brit Chadasha is equally clear—as long as the reader adheres to the interpretive principles outlined above. As far as Sha'ul's writings are concerned, most if not all of his exhortations on everyday living—in Jewish thinking, his *halacha*—are based on teachings from the Torah.

Moreover, we need to consider what Ya'acov (James) wrote to the Jewish believers in the diaspora. In his letter, he strongly urges them to follow Torah. Notice particularly what he says in 1:22–25. He likens the person who does not follow the Word of God to someone who looks into a mirror, walks away, and forgets what he looks like! When the natural man looks in a literal mirror, he sees a reflection of his physical being. When a new creation in Messiah looks into the perfect Torah (Ya'acov's language), he sees in its laws, decrees, commandments, judgments, and teachings a reflection of his new-creation self. This brings us to our next characteristic of Torah.

The Torah Reflects God's
Holiness, Goodness, and Righteousness

Rav Sha'ul set out to teach that the failure of the Torah to produce justification arises from man's misuse of it, not from any deficiency in the teachings themselves. As he points out in Romans 7:12, "So then, the Torah is holy, and the command is holy, and righteous, and good." We need to let ourselves feel the full impact of this verse. There are some who say that Romans 7 is talking about the end of the Torah. They assert that when Messiah came, we died to the Torah as if it were like a spouse who had died. Then, they contend, since the Torah is dead, we are now free to be "married" to Messiah.

How can the Torah be both dead to us and at the same time holy, righteous, and good? When Sha'ul writes, "We died to the law" (Romans 7:4), he is referring to the reality that we have ceased to relate to the Torah in our former legalistic manner. Having died to that thinking and behavior, we are now free to live a life of grace, expressing God's Torah through Messiah.

What has changed is our relationship to the Torah. Before we were redeemed, the Torah condemned us for our sin and taught us about Messiah. If we attempted to follow the Torah or to participate in the Torah observant community, the Torah may also have helped to protect us until we reached the Teacher. But when we met the Teacher, the Messiah, everything changed. We died (Galatians 2:19–20)! In our new relationship with Him came a new relationship to Torah as well.

We can now confirm with Sha'ul that for us as believers, the Torah is holy, righteous and good. The words of the Torah are now our life (Deuteronomy 32:47). When we study Torah, we can learn a great deal about God Himself and His eternal attributes. And when we practice Torah, we are practicing that which is holy, righteous and good. We are also participating in our new life—the life of God.

Life's Built-in Reminders

The Torah lifestyle is brilliantly designed by God Himself according to His perfect knowledge of how we function as spiritual beings—seated in Messiah in the heavenlies, yet living on the earth. We need to be reminded continually of this glorious truth, because the "cares of this world" are always seeking to distract us from it. The Torah lifestyle was designed with built-in reminders of God's truths, helping us to remember our identity both as new creations in Messiah and as members of the redeemed and holy community.

A Jewish Reminder

There are several ways in which the Torah functions as a reminder. First, it reminds Jewish people what it means to be Jewish. Perhaps you are a Messianic Jew. Because of the excellent training in many fellowships on what it means to be "Messianic," there is little need to define this concept here.

But if we claim to be Messianic *Jews*, what does the "Jewish" part mean? Does being Jewish mean having an Israeli identification card, or a membership in the local Jewish Community Center? What defines Jewishness? There is only one authoritative place where we can learn and be continually reminded of our biblical Jewishness. This is in the Torah. As Orthodox Israeli Rabbi Shlomo Riskin so aptly put it: "A Jewishness without Torah is an impossibility, a term devoid of meaning."[7]

Let us clarify. There is a difference between being a Jewish person and living out our Jewishness. One's birth and ancestry determine whether one is Jewish or not. But only the Torah can define what Jewishness means, how to live out our Jewish birth.

Perhaps a slight change of terms may help to clarify the issue. The Bible says that Abraham was called a Hebrew. Although there is some difference of opinion, the word *Hebrew* most likely means "one who has crossed over"—from the root *avar* (עבר).[8] God calls him a Hebrew because he crossed over from his former geographical area to reach the land of Canaan. But God also intends for us to learn that a Hebrew is one who has crossed over from his former life (in this case one of idolatry) to the new life into which God has called him. Knowing this may shed new light on the biblical reference to Abraham as "our father." Literally, he is the father of all of his physical descendants. But he is also the father of all who have crossed over spiritually, from darkness into the wonderful light of belief in the one true God, as He has revealed Himself.

To be sure, the Brit Chadasha continues the biblical definition of being Jewish. Rav Sha'ul clearly states the Torah definition and clarifies it. In Romans 2:28–29, he writes, "For he is not a Jew who is one outwardly; neither is circumcision that which is outward in the flesh. But he is a Jew who is one inwardly; and circumcision is that which is of the heart, by the Spirit, not by the letter; and his praise is not from men, but from God." In other words, he is not denying the fact that a Jewish person is one by physical birth. But—understanding our definition of a Hebrew—he says that real Jewishness, or being a Hebrew, involves being born that way not just physically, but also spiritually, by the Spirit of God. The Torah (as well as the Brit Chadasha) adds meat to that definition and reminds us of what a Hebrew looks like.

There are other believers in Yeshua who were not born physical descendants of Abraham. Concerning these believers we are told,

> Even so Abraham believed God, and it was reckoned to him as righteousness. Therefore, be sure that it is those who are of faith who are sons of Abraham. And the Scripture, foreseeing that God would justify the Gentiles by faith, preached the gospel beforehand to Abraham, saying, "All the nations shall be blessed in you." So then those who are of faith are blessed with Abraham, the believer. (Galatians 3:6-9)

Thus, in a spiritual sense, non-Jewish believers in Yeshua are also Hebrews, those who have crossed over like their spiritual father Abraham. It does not mean that they are Jewish people. It means that because they are both grafted in to Israel and share in the faith of Israel, they are like their father Abraham, having crossed over into God's call for their life by trusting in the Messiah of Israel.

For such (as well as the "natural branches," Jewish people by birth) the Torah also serves as a book of reminders. Reminders of what? Reminders that we are the people of God, the "called-out ones"—those who have crossed over. Let us see how this works.

We have already seen in the writings of Ya'acov that the Word of God is our mirror. One of the reasons we do not follow the Word is because we forget who we are! Accordingly, one of the greatest gifts God has given us is a lifestyle that helps us to remember—to remember the truth, to remember righteousness, and to remember who we are as new creations in Messiah.

The Torah describes a lifestyle of built-in daily, weekly, monthly, and yearly reminders. If we embrace the Torah, it will help us to live our lives in continual remembrance of who God called us to be. Let us look at some practical examples. As we go through some illustrations, try to catch a glimpse of this incredible gift from your all-knowing, all-loving, all-merciful and gracious God.

A Daily Reminder—The *Tzitziot*

Numbers 15:37–40 talks about one of the daily reminders found in the Torah. Each morning as we don our prayer shawl, we notice the fringe, or *tzitzit* (plural, *tzitziot*), hanging from each of its four corners—each with its specified blue cord. The Torah instructs us, "and you shall have the fringe, that you may look upon it and remember…." Remember, that is, to behave consistently with who you now are. We are no longer slaves in Egypt, but a royal priesthood, a holy nation.

As we put on our tzitziot, it can be helpful to pray along the following lines:

> We are a chosen people, a royal priesthood, a holy nation, a people belonging to God, that we may declare the praises of Him who called us out of darkness into His wonderful light. (I Peter 1:9) For the lips of a priest ought to preserve knowledge, and from his mouth men should seek instruction—because he is the messenger of the Lord Almighty. (Malachi 2:7)

> Abba, as I put on these tzitziot as You have commanded, may I be reminded of who I am and my

purpose upon the earth. As I look upon the fringes of my garment today, may I truly be reminded to be a doer of Your Word and not a hearer only. May the words of my mouth and the meditations of my heart be acceptable to You, O God, my Rock and my Redeemer. You have written Your Torah upon my heart and my mind. Now may I walk in and yield my members to Messiah in me, the hope of glory. I am consecrated to you, O God. As I look upon this blue cord this day, may I be reminded that I am one of Your Royal Priesthood, that I may not allow the world, the flesh, or the evil one to rule over me.

These final blessings are especially appropriate for putting on the *tallit*, or prayer shawl. Unfold the tallit, hold it in readiness to wrap around yourself, and recite the following:

Blessed are You, O Lord our God, King of the universe, who has sanctified us with Your commandments and commanded us to wrap ourselves in the tzitziot. Amen.

Wrap the tallit around your body and head, then recite:

How precious is Your kindness, O God! The sons of man take refuge in the shadow of Your wings. May they be seated from the abundance of Your house; and may You give them to drink from the stream of Your delights. For with You is the source of life—by Your light we shall see light. Extend Your kindness to those who know You, and Your charity to the upright of heart.

A Weekly Reminder—The Shabbat

How would you like to be given the gift of one day each week when you would not have to do all your regular daily work? You would have time to read and think about all of the following magnificent truths:

I am a new creation in the Messiah. (I Corinthians 5:17)

My sins are fully atoned for. (Romans 5:12–21; 8:28–30)

My old man is dead and buried. (Romans 6)

I am justified and redeemed. (Romans 3:24)

I am no longer condemned. (Romans 8:1)

I am sanctified, holy, set apart. (I Corinthians 1)

I am the righteousness of God. (II Corinthians 5:21)

I am chosen, holy, and blameless. (Ephesians 1:4)

I am alive! (Ephesians 2:5)

I am seated in the heavenly places. (Ephesians 2:6)

I am created for good works, prepared beforehand that I should walk in them. (Ephesians 2:10)

Being reminded of who I now am (through the mirror of James 1:22–25), I have a given day without pressure to practice living out who I am and not who I used to be. Unrestricted by the regular demanding activities of the weekday, my mind can be set on truth and on practicing these truths. I have time and energy to practice the truth.

In light of these thoughts, come to know the Shabbat rest spoken of as the true Good News in Hebrews 4. The redemptive work of Messiah in your life is a finished work. Who we once were is now dead and buried. We are now the righteousness of God in Messiah, a totally new creation. Know who you are! It *is* good news! "There remains therefore a Sabbath rest for the people of God. For the one who has entered His rest has himself also rested from his works, as God did from His." (Hebrews 4:9–11) In order for us to rest in the same way as God did, we have to discover from the Word in what way God did rest. We see in Bereshit (Genesis) 2:1–3 that God *ceased* from His work. The Hebrew word translated "ceased" is *shavat* (שבת), the word from which we get the term "Shabbat." Thus, the Torah tells us how God rests from His work.

Take a closer look at this passage. What does verse 1 say about God's creation? That it was finished in all its vast array. In verse 2, why did God cease from all His work of creating? Because it was a finished work, a completed work. Was there anything left to be done? Was anything left to be added? No! All that was left for God to do was to stop working and enjoy all that He had done.

The message of the Good News is that we may now rest from "our own work," in the same way that God rested from His (Hebrews 4:10). The whole of our life, prior to the day of our salvation, was our "six days of labor"—trying to measure up, trying to attain to our own standards and belief system of righteousness (Romans 10:3). Then we entered our "seventh day." We entered the Shabbat rest of the Good News, and now are called to live the remainder of our days in that seventh day, choosing to cease from all works of the flesh. "For it is no longer I who live, but Messiah who lives in me; and the life I live in the body I live by faith [taking God at His Word] in the Son of God, who loved me and gave Himself for me." (Galatians 2:20)

Do we find it difficult—perhaps nearly impossible—to remember these truths on Sunday? How about on Tuesday? Could it be that we *need* the gift of one day out of seven set apart as a practice day? A day to be in remembrance of who we are, to practice these truths as we relate to others—the words that we speak, the walk we walk?

That gift is Shabbat, one of the central teachings of the Torah. This is the weekly reminder! Now let us take a look at the wonderful promises found in Isaiah 58:13–14.

> If you keep your feet from breaking the Sabbath and
> from doing as you please on My holy day, if you call

the Sabbath a delight and the Lord's holy day honorable, and if you honor it by not going your own way and not doing as you please or speaking idle words, then you will find your joy in the Lord, and I will cause you to ride on the heights of the land and to feast on the inheritance of your father Jacob. The mouth of the Lord has spoken! (NIV)

It is important to note that in verse 13, where the NIV reads "if you honor it by not going your own way," the word "it" does not appear in the original Hebrew. Rather, it should be translated *Him,* meaning God.

One of the main results of celebrating the Shabbat in this way is that, over time, we will find ourselves capable of walking more and more in our new man. In this we will find our joy in the Lord.

Monthly Reminders

What about the monthly reminders? The women of the redeemed community have many wonderful callings and gifts which serve the whole community. One very special calling is experienced by those of menstruating age. In *Vayikra* (Leviticus) 15:19–24, God gives very descriptive instructions about the menstruation process. The woman's body is designed to picture the body of Messiah, prepared to bring forth life. During the childbearing years, the female body prepares each month to bring forth life. When life does not occur, however, the lining of the uterus sheds itself, resulting in the menstrual flow. The Torah describes such a woman as being in a state of *niddah.* The instructions given in Torah concerning this seven-day period form a vital monthly teaching reminder.

In the Jewish community, the teachings found in Leviticus 15:19–24 are called niddah, which means that during her monthly menstruation a woman is declared to be "impure."

She remains in this state for a period of seven days, at the end of which she goes to the *mikvah*. (For those unfamiliar with the term, the mikvah is simply an immersion pool.) When she emerges, she is declared "pure." What does this mean? Was she in sin? Did she do something wrong to be considered impure? How is it that simply passing through the mikvah made her pure again?

There was no sin involved. God has called women to live a special teaching reminder of a crucial truth within the redeemed community, one that must be repeated each and every month. Here's how the teaching picture works:

As a new creation in Messiah, we are created to bring forth His life in how we live. Insofar as we do this, we are *tahor* (טהור), or pure (Torah teaching: that which is of life is pure). If we enter a time of walking in the flesh, then during that period we do not bring forth life. Not bringing forth life is death, which is impure, or *tamei* (טמא). When we realize we have been walking in the flesh and confess our sin, we come to the end of that impure period.

All we need to do in order to walk in the place of life again is to know ourselves in the "Mikvah." Messiah Himself is our Mikvah. In Him we are pure, able to let His life come forth through us again. It is a monthly reminder of the seriousness of sin: when I am impure, everything I touch becomes impure. It is also a reminder that, as a new creation, I have only to confess my sin, know myself pure in the Messiah, and keep walking.

We need to be reminded often of how serious a transgression it is to walk in the flesh rather than in the newness of life. Without this monthly reminder, we pay the price of forgetfulness in regard to this truth, one that is so central to our walk of faith.

Annual Reminders

Some of God's reminders arise on a yearly basis. For example, He commanded Israel to observe the *Mo'adim*—the cycle of Holy Days found in Leviticus 23—to help them remember the great things He has done for them. By living out this annual cycle, Israel would always keep in mind their former slavery, and what God did to redeem them and set them free.

Since, therefore, there are appointed times when Israel is to remember their historical redemption, these times can also serve as special reminders of God's redemptive truths. Year by year, all the doctrines of our faith are kept before us as we celebrate them individually and as a body. As this is done, special provision is made for us to participate in these truths. Celebrating our victory in the Messiah is built in to the Torah lifestyle.

Look, for example, at some of the important doctrines which each Holy Day brings to our attention:

Pesach (Passover)—redemption, salvation, deliverance, freedom

Unleavened Bread—sanctification

Counting the Days (Counting the "Omer")—sanctification, deliverance

Shavuot (Pentecost)—the Word of God, the Spirit of God, firstfruits, ecclesiology

Yom Teruah (Feast of the Shofar)—eschatology

Yom Kippur (Day of Atonement)—atonement, forgiveness, blood sacrifices

Succot (Feast of Tabernacles)—worship, praise, redemption, eschatology, thanksgiving, celebrating the harvest of righteousness in our lives

All of these doctrines, introduced in the Torah, see their full development in the Brit Chadasha. We refer to this as "progressive revelation." The Torah makes provision for the corporate expression of these concepts through the Holy Day cycle. This annual cycle, therefore, is a yearly way to remember these doctrines.

We have only mentioned a few of the many daily, weekly, monthly, and yearly reminders that are built in to the biblical Torah lifestyle. We encourage you to read through the Torah week by week, following the traditional *parashiot* (weekly Torah portions as read in the synagogue). Watch for these reminders as you do so, viewing them as gifts from God which help us to remember Him and what He has done for us. (A schedule of the weekly portions appears at the end of this book.)

God designed the Torah lifestyle in such a way as to remind us continually that salvation is His work alone, from start to finish. It is His desire that, remembering this, we might participate in the truth by faith. How do we do this? By living the Torah lifestyle. As it is written in James 2:18, "I show you my faith by what I do!"

Chapter Four
For Me? For You? For Who?

For Me? For You? For Who?

The material in this book has been, so far, relatively simple—but critical. For without first establishing the nature of Torah, it is impossible to define the ways in which it should be applied. To determine who should follow the Torah is a gigantic undertaking. It is also an extremely controversial exercise, as there are many different viewpoints on the subject. In light of this, please understand that we intend to be as gracious as possible concerning the different, sometimes opposing positions set forth in this chapter. Our goal is to study how much of the Torah should be followed—and by whom.

(Please note that the following is an overview of ideas, not of movements or specific teachers. Hence, there are no formal labels attached to these ideas. Furthermore, as we are writing, for the most part, to believers in Yeshua, we will state only those viewpoints which have relevance to them.)

Idea 1:
Torah Should Not Be Followed

There are well-meaning believers who suggest that the Torah is an antiquated document, that its precepts were for a particular people—the Israelites—and for a particular time frame, the age or dispensation of law. Therefore, they say, the Torah should no longer be followed. An example of this standpoint is contained in the following quotation from Arnold Fruchtenbaum's book, *Israelology*:

> The clear-cut teaching of the New Testament is that the law of Moses has been rendered inoperative with the death of Christ; in other words, the law in its totality no longer has authority over any individual.[9]

Not for Salvation

This position, so aptly captured by Fruchtenbaum, is based on a faulty assumption about the nature and purposes of Torah. Obedience to the Torah of Moshe was *never* intended to provide or maintain salvation. It simply is not a salvation document. One can, through a proper understanding of the Torah, learn about entering a relationship with the Lord by His grace through faith. But God never gave the document for the purpose of granting salvation through its obedience.

There are some passages in the Brit Chadasha which, at first glance, appear to support Fruchtenbaum's position. For example, Hebrews 8:7 says, "For if the first covenant had been faultless, there would have been no occasion sought for a second." Verse 13 continues this argument: "When He said, 'A new covenant,' He has made the first one obsolete. But whatever is becoming obsolete and growing old is ready to disappear."

At face value, the teaching of these verses would appear to be devastating to any who hold that the Torah should be followed in this day and age. However, closer examination may reveal a different conclusion.

First, it is important to note the context of these verses. This passage is couched directly in the middle of a section of Hebrews discussing the sacrificial/priestly system. Central to the covenant with Moshe was the system of atonement, which involved the use of sacrificial animals and a special class of workers called priests. The Book of Hebrews was written to Jewish believers to show them that *this one aspect* of that covenant was in the process of changing. Its glaring message is that Yeshua of Nazareth, the Messiah, is the end or culmination of that particular system. His death was the final, once-for-all atonement for sin, through His blood, which He offered on the altar in the heavenly *mishkan* (the tabernacle).

A second observation concerns itself with the words, "But whatever is becoming obsolete and growing old is ready to disappear." When the Book of Hebrews was written, there were at least two (possibly three, if we count the Samaritans) Jewish priestly systems in operation. The most well known of these, maintained by the Sadducees, centered around the Second Temple in Jerusalem. This is the one mentioned most frequently in the Brit Chadasha.

Not all, however, were in support of that Temple and its system. Consequently, there was a second Jewish priestly/sacrificial system, operated by the Dead Sea (Qumran) community, which was in fierce opposition to the Jerusalem Sadducean Temple system. No matter which system was considered more valid, both were a testimony that the sacrificial system was alive and well in the early first century CE and during the time when Hebrews was most likely written.

This situation changed drastically when Yeshua died. The gospels attest that upon His death, the veil separating the holy place from the Holy of Holies in the Second Temple was ripped in half (Matthew 27:51). This was an obvious indication from HaShem that no matter what sacrifices were offered in the Temple, they would be rendered redundant, because the real sacrifice had taken place in the death of Yeshua.

Keep in mind, however, that God did not destroy the Temple. Its sacrifices continued for approximately 40 years after Yeshua returned to heaven. Neither did He destroy the Dead Sea community during that time. Both continued until the First Jewish Revolt (68–73 CE), which indicates that these systems were still in operation at the time the Jewish believers were reading the Book of Hebrews. It can be said, therefore, that because the vestiges of the older covenant were still functioning they were not finished. Instead, they were "becoming obsolete and growing old." But only the sacrificial system! In other words, this verse says very little about the whole of Torah, but much about the specific instructions in Torah concerning the sacrifices.[10]

We would like to mention one further detail concerning these verses. Hebrews 8:7 implies that the older covenant was imperfect. A faultless one was needed. This does not mean that *everything* about the older covenant was imperfect. For example, is there something imperfect about Succot? If so, perhaps someone should have informed the prophet Zechariah before he told us that the whole world would celebrate Succot after Messiah's return! In addition to Succot, Isaiah 2:3 says that in the Messianic kingdom it will be the Torah which will go forth from Zion. How could something as "imperfect" as Torah be part of Messiah's kingdom?

What was imperfect was not the covenant as a whole, nor even most of its specific provisions—it was the sacrificial system! Animal sacrifices could only cover sin temporarily.

For this reason, Yom Kippur was observed every year. But Hebrews teaches us that the faultless sacrifice of Yeshua replaced that imperfect sacrificial system.

"Law versus Grace"

The belief that Torah should no longer be followed often stems from a misunderstanding concerning the nature of the document itself. It is correct to observe that one biblical purpose of the Torah was to "prove the sinfulness of man."[11] However, there are more biblical purposes for the Torah than to point out our wrongdoing.

In addition, some scholars do not adhere to the basic definition of the Hebrew word *torah* as meaning "teaching." Instead, they have translated it as "law." The Greek word used to translate the Hebrew text in the Septuagint is, indeed, usually rendered "law." But this does not mean it should be translated as such in every instance of the biblical text, especially in the Brit Chadasha. Rabbi Eckstein confirms this when he states, "The term Torah has a variety of connotations. Etymologically, it means 'teachings,' not 'law,' as it is so often mistranslated."[12]

This translation problem, then, has given rise to a fabricated theological dichotomy in many Christian circles. Oftentimes, this dichotomy is called "law versus grace," or a similar formulation. Based on this, some theologians pit Torah against the concept of "grace," as if the two are opposed to each other. This problematic theological formulation results in statements such as the following: "With the coming of Christ, grace as a rule of life superseded law as a rule of life."[13] Declarations of this type have gone a long way to influence many believers against Torah.

To be sure, if Torah was against grace, then perhaps the above statement would be true. But Torah does not oppose grace. If we adhere to the proper definition of Torah as "teaching" as opposed to "law," then pronouncements such as the one quoted above are very unfortunate and should be avoided. Let it be stated emphatically: it is man's mishandling, misinterpreting, and misuse of Torah which causes it to be against grace—not the document itself!

Idea 2:
Only Certain Parts of Torah Should be Followed

Some would rather not throw out the baby with the bath water, so to speak. They are not willing to say that Torah in its entirety should *not* be followed; neither, however, are they willing to say that it should. Those who hold to this viewpoint sometimes speak of Torah in terms of a threefold division: civil, ceremonial and ethical. The civil sections of the Torah are those dealing with governmental functions, such as the teachings concerning capital punishment and other jurisprudence functions. The ceremonial sections concern the sacrifices, the priesthood, and everything connected with these institutions. The ethical laws are those which govern how a person lives his everyday life in relationship to his fellow man.

There is a certain degree of merit to this point of view. No matter how we understand certain passages in the Book of Hebrews, it is clear that the book singles out at least one separate category of Torah, the "ceremonial." In addition, there are also specific parts of the Torah which are applicable only to those who live in the land of Israel.

However, when we begin to dissect Torah in a way that was never intended, hermeneutic difficulties inevitably arise. Remember that Torah is a covenant. It is intended to be understood as a whole. For example, is it really fair to the Torah to say that one will only follow the ethical sections, while ignoring the civil? More important, does Torah itself give us the right to make such distinctions? The only exception is that made by the Brit Chadasha itself: the sacrifices would no longer be necessary.

Idea 3:
All of Torah is to be Followed—
But Not Necessarily by Physical Israel

Some theologians say that all of the Torah should be obeyed, but that the ones who are to do it are the Church—which, they say, has theologically replaced Israel. Of course, in regard to the teachings concerning the sacrifices, they recognize that in Messiah these came to completion. Nevertheless, they maintain that it is incumbent upon believers to follow the rest of Torah.

By suggesting that the Church has replaced Israel, adherents to this viewpoint have already revealed their basic method of hermeneutics: spiritualization. They have given up the fundamental, literal interpretation of the Bible in lieu of a symbolic, spiritual or allegorical one. This viewpoint has characterized most of the Church since the middle of the second century, and continues to plague a good portion of it—even some of the believing, evangelical Church—to this very day.

To be sure, those who subscribe to this viewpoint are consistent: just as they transform literal physical Israel into the Church, so also do they spiritualize many of the specific teachings of the Torah. For example, we have met a number of people who hold to this viewpoint, and have read some of their writings. We have yet to meet one who wears fringes according to Numbers 15. Moreover, we have not met one who faithfully keeps the Holy Day cycle of Leviticus 23. Somehow, these parts of Torah are spiritualized to mean something else and, therefore, not followed.

We believe that this method of interpretation is not consistent with the proper exegesis of the Scriptures. Specifically, Romans 11 makes a clear distinction between non-Jewish believers in Yeshua and physical Israel. It clearly asserts that there is still a future plan for physical Israel. Yes, there are allegories and spiritualization within the Bible, but the use of such figurative language must be governed by recognizing its proper place within the literal, grammatical, historical method of interpretation. Hence, through consistent use of a literal method of Scripture interpretation, we can easily lay to rest such theories as the replacement of Israel by the Church.

Idea 4:
Torah is Applicable Today to Israel and to All So Inclined

We come now to our last category. This is the opinion that Torah is to be followed by believers—especially Jewish believers in Yeshua—in this day and age.

First and Foremost, the Remnant

In the foundational chapters of this book, we demonstrated the unique relationship between the Torah and the physical nation of Israel. The Torah is Israel's national constitution, sacred marriage ketubah, and its solemn covenant with God. There is no indication in the Scriptures that this special relationship has ended. The establishment of the Brit Chadasha, like the addition of the other covenants, did not abrogate its predecessors; it only affirmed, strengthened, and complemented them. This is the thrust of Sha'ul's argument in Galatians 3, especially when he asks, "Is the Torah then contrary to the promises of God? May it never be!" (Galatians 3:21)

The Accusation Against Sha'ul

The Jewish believers of the first century understood this truth as well. Acts 21 recounts a remarkable incident in Sha'ul's life which illustrates this. Returning from a journey during which he had shared the Good News with the Gentiles, Sha'ul found himself confronted by the Jerusalem leadership. It was rumored, they said, that he had been "teaching all the Jews who are among the Gentiles to forsake Moshe, telling them not to circumcise their children, nor to walk according to the customs." (Acts 21:21) Now the leaders wanted to know: Were these accusations true or false?

Not long before this meeting, Sha'ul had written to the believers in Galatia and Rome. They were confused by some of the difficult things he had written concerning Torah. Now, face to face with the Rabbi, they wanted to know the truth of the matter: "Do you follow Torah or not? Do you approve of other Jewish believers' following the Torah?" In other words, is it still valid to follow the Torah as a Jewish believer in Yeshua?

This was Rav Sha'ul's big moment. Because of his influence as the greatest theologian the body of Messiah ever had (next to Yeshua), what he would say or do at this moment was of crucial importance. It would determine the proper interpretation of the confusing statements in his letters concerning Torah. It would also set a precedent for other Jewish believers to follow.

So what happened? The elders gave him the option of disproving the allegations by paying for four of them who had taken the Nazirite vow as described in Numbers 6. Not only was he to pay their expenses, but also to go through a purification immersion along with them. Much to the shame of many a modern-day evangelical theologian, he did just as he was asked (verse 26).

What Sha'ul had done was to make a statement which should have been echoed throughout the centuries: "Torah is for today! Jewish believers should be taught and encouraged to follow the Torah of Moshe!" Many may not appreciate this conclusion, but the Greek in verse 20 tells us that there were tens of thousands of Messianic Jewish people in Jerusalem "who have believed, and they are all zealous for the Torah."

Four Centuries Later

Life was not easy for the early Jewish believers. Because of their trust in Yeshua, they suffered persecution at the hands of traditional Jews. Moreover, because of their adherence to the covenant of Sinai, they would also eventually suffer persecution from other believers in Yeshua. After what is generally referred to as the Second Jewish Revolt (the actual second revolt took place in Alexandria, Cyremaica and Cyprus) against Rome failed miserably in 135 CE, many Church leaders and preachers made a concentrated effort to rid the Church of any Jewish trappings. Needless to say, it was the Messianic Jewish observance of Torah that brought the persecution from fellow believers.

Not everyone gave in to the pressure, however. There existed from the earliest days a remnant of Jewish believers who were true to the covenant. In Church history, this group is called the Nazarenes. When we were in Bible college and seminary, very little was taught concerning the Nazarenes. They were portrayed as a group of Jewish believers who, unfortunately, still clung to the "law of Moses."

A more accurate picture is painted by scholar Dr. Ray Pritz, who wrote his doctoral dissertation on this group. He writes, "There emerges from our considerations an entity, a viable entity of law-keeping Christians of Jewish background. These were direct descendants of the first Jewish believers in Jesus." Moreover, the Nazarenes did not "accept as binding on themselves (or on any Jews) the oral law as embodied in the Mishnah. Their Christology too called Christ the Son of God. And finally, this group had not lost hope that the Jewish people might yet turn to accept Jesus as the Messiah."[14]

Both the Nazarenes and their predecessors, the Jewish believers of whom we read in the Book of Acts, serve as illustrations that, biblically, Jewish believers in Yeshua have always had a special relationship to the Torah. They were chosen to follow it.

The remnant of Torah-observant Jewish believers lasted until sometime near the end of the fourth century, when Torah-keeping Jewish believers in Yeshua somehow left the pages of history. Today, another Jewish revival is taking place. More and more Jewish believers in Yeshua are learning the importance of living according to the national covenant of our people, the Torah.

An Amended Covenant

How much of the Torah can be followed? The Book of Hebrews provides part of the answer for us. In Hebrews 8–10, we are told that the older covenant has certainly been modified, but not done away with! The Brit Chadasha clearly teaches that God does not require us to bring a lamb to our temple. Yeshua is the sacrificial atonement.

There are many historical examples of covenants and national constitutions being modified or amended. The first set of amendments to the United States Constitution is called the Bill of Rights. If the Constitution is amended, does that mean that Americans should not follow the "old" Constitution? Of course not! It is still in force, and citizens of the USA have a special relationship to it which people from other lands do not enjoy.

Let us carry this idea over to the Brit Chadasha. The New Covenant did not nullify the covenant on Sinai, but simply amended it. In fact, a good linguistic case can be made concerning the Hebrew verb for "new," *chadash* (חדש). It is the same word that is used for the renewal of the moon every thirty days. This is called a month. In Hebrew, "month" and "new" contain the same root, chadash. What happens? Do we get a brand new moon, freshly created every month? No! The appearance of the moon is merely *renewed*. Carrying this concept over to the word "new," the New Covenant is not a brand-new, freshly drawn agreement. Rather, it is merely a covenant *renewal*, complete with the appropriate amendments and signs of ratification. Thus, all the regulations concerning the sacrificial/priestly system have been amended. Consequently, they are not to be followed.

Divine Permission

As we begin this difficult discussion, we would like to make two qualifying statements. The first concerns the motivations of the individual in following the Torah. Plainly stated, we believe that no one, Jewish or non-Jewish, may earn, merit, or keep his eternal salvation by following the Torah. The second qualifying statement is that, in this whole discussion of the non-Jewish person's relationship to the Torah, we have purposely avoided the words "must" and "should," as the use of these words tends to cloud the issues at hand no matter to whom we are referring.

Now, how can we engage in a meaningful exploration of this subject without once employing these words? We can begin by examining the implication of a series of biblical passages which directly relate to this subject: that at the very least, the relationship of the non-Jewish person to the Torah is one of permission and encouragement.

What About All Those People?

By the grace of God, we received an overwhelmingly favorable response to our first edition of *Torah Rediscovered*. But this response came from some very unexpected quarters. We anticipated that the book would be read and considered in Messianic Jewish circles. What we could not have predicted was the startlingly positive response from those who cannot be classified as Messianic Jews. We are referring to believers in fellowships, home study groups, and churches which traditionally have not embraced the viewpoints on the Torah espoused by this book. Moreover, we have been impressed at the sheer numbers of people responding to this message. Many evangelicals, charismatic and otherwise, are hungry to know more about the Torah. Beyond that, however, many of these have expressed a deep desire, not only to know the Torah, but also to learn to follow it.

What should we say to such people? More important, what would the Holy One say to them? To answer this, we need to look into His Word. Following are several passages of Scripture which have one thing in common: all have something to teach us about the relationship of non-Israelites to the Torah of Israel. Even though these passages come from quite diverse locations in the Scriptures, we will strive to avoid violating their context and intended meaning. We submit these teachings for your prayerful consideration.

Our Father Abraham

Abraham was not a Jewish person. He was born a Gentile in the city of Ur of the Chaldeans, a city in Mesopotamia. We are not certain how he came to believe in the one true God, the Creator of heaven and earth, the God of his descendants (Israel). But as we read about him in the pages of Genesis, we find a Gentile who had a profound relationship with God.

It is true that Abraham was the father of the Jewish people. But he himself was not born Jewish. Judaism began with Abraham when God entered into a covenant, signified by circumcision, with him and his progeny.

Abraham lived several hundred years before one of his descendants, Moshe, would receive the Torah on Mount Sinai. Yet the Lord said of him, "Abraham heard My voice and guarded My commandments, My statutes, and My Torah." (Genesis 26:5) Actually, the Hebrew is even more emphatic: "Abraham heard My voice and guarded My protective guards, My commandments, My statutes, and My Torah."

How did Abraham do this before the Torah, the mitzvot, and the chukim were revealed to Moshe? How did he come to call upon the name of the Lord? How did he know, as his ancestor Noach (Noah) knew, that to relate properly to the Lord required a blood sacrifice? Could it be that the Lord Himself somehow revealed to these non-Jewish men of God portions of His holy Torah, in the expectation that they would receive this teaching as His Word to them?

Israel Was to Attract the Gentiles

Let us travel onward in history, to the time when Abraham's physical family, the children of Israel, were camping on the plains of the Jordan Valley opposite Jericho and preparing to take possession of the Promised Land.

The Lord had called this nation to be separate and holy unto Him. They were to live the Torah before the surrounding nations as a mighty witness of the true God: who He was, and how He desired His people to relate to Him. God equipped Israel for this task in many ways. For example, He chose to situate the nation at the crossroads of the world! The Promised Land was an ancient and natural land bridge between

Japan, India and China in the Far East, Africa in the south, and Europe in the north. Accordingly, many of antiquity's most traveled trade routes traversed the land of Israel. Because of this, the Israelites had ample exposure to people from all nations of the then-known world.

Furthermore, the Holy One provided Israel with the Torah. This body of writing contained provisions and instructions for relating properly to God, living peacefully with others, and finding prosperity in the Land. If Israel had made the Torah their national lifestyle in the way God intended, all nations of the earth would have discovered this life and flocked to Israel's God—the one true God. As we read in the Torah itself:

> See, I have taught you decrees and laws as the Lord my God commanded me, so that you may follow them in the land you are entering to take possession of it. Observe them carefully, for this will show your wisdom and understanding to the nations, who will hear about all these decrees and say, "Surely this great nation is a wise and understanding people." What other nation is so great as to have their gods near them the way the Lord our God is near us whenever we pray to Him? And what other nation is so great as to have such righteous decrees and laws as this body of laws I am setting before you today? (Deuteronomy 4:5–8)

Suppose, for a moment, that it had worked! Suppose that some Gentile people groups had observed the wisdom of Israel's God as expressed through their living out of the Torah. And that, provoked to jealousy, they had chosen to embrace the God of Israel. What then? Would Israel have said to these non-Jews, "You can have our God, but not our Torah?" That would be ludicrous! The text in Genesis clearly implies that to accept Israel's God also meant to live by the revealed wisdom of His Torah.

The Prophets Made Provision for Gentiles

Let us continue again through the centuries, to approximately 700 BCE. When Isaiah, one of Israel's greatest prophets, wrote his book, he did so with the intention of admonishing Israel and Judah to forsake their sins and to live by the Covenant of the Torah. He also encouraged the faithful remnant of believers to continue in their faith in the Lord.

However, Isaiah had a message for the Gentiles as well. He had words of rebuke and warning for them, as chapters 13–23 indicate. However, particularly in chapter 56, we also find words of encouragement for the remnant of Gentiles who followed the God of Israel. Indeed, for our purposes this is a most remarkable passage, meriting our close attention.

Chapter 56 of Isaiah opens up with an encouragement to the remnant of Israel to continue following the Covenant of Torah. The prophet calls upon them to "maintain justice and do what is right" as well as to "keep the Shabbat." These are words which we might expect a prophet of Israel or Judah to speak to the Jewish people. Notice, however, who Isaiah is addressing in verses 3 and 6. He speaks about "the foreigner"—but not just any foreigner. These are *foreigners who have bound themselves to the Lord.* In other words, the prophet has some important things to say to non-Jewish believers.

First, Isaiah tells these non-Israelites (non-Jewish believers) that the Lord Himself will make certain to *include* them with the remnant of His people among Israel. This is the thrust of 56:3.

Second, presumably because these Gentile believers share a portion with Israel, Isaiah reminds them that the Lord will grant them access to "My holy mountain" and that He will accept their offerings at the temple, because "My house shall be called a house of prayer for all nations." (In the Hebrew, the word translated "nations" is *amim*—literally, "peoples.") In other words, God was doing all He could to assure these non-Israelite believers that they were on *equal* footing with Israel, the people of the covenant. Yet He refers to them not as Israel, but as "foreigners!"

Third, notice how Isaiah describes the lifestyle of these Gentile believers. He characterizes them in verse 6 as people "who keep the Shabbat without desecrating it and who hold fast to My covenant." This is an utterly remarkable statement to make about believers not born physically into the nation of Israel. It implies that although they cannot be called "Jews" because of their birth, yet because of their relationship with the Lord they are entitled to follow Torah—and even encouraged in their observance! In addition, they are described as participants in "the covenant."

Finally, in verse 8, Isaiah prophesies about the generations to come. He looks beyond his present situation and says, "The Sovereign Lord declares—He who gathers the exiles of Israel: I will gather still others to them besides those already gathered." At the very least, the Lord was promising that many from among the nations would believe in Him, thereby becoming a part of "them"—Israel—which would include living by the Torah! When would this happen? The natural answer to this would be at the ingathering of the Gentiles described in the Book of Acts.

Yeshua Introduces the Torah to the Nations

Just before He went back to His Father's throne from whence He came, the Messiah gave careful instructions for his *talmidim* to follow. He told them in Matthew 28:19–20: "As you are going, make disciples from all nations, immersing them in the name of the Father and of the Son, and of the Spirit of God."

This passage, often referred to as the "great commission" by many believers, contains several points frequently overlooked by sincere Bible teachers in the churches. The first is the nature of the material Yeshua's followers were to teach to the potential believers from the Gentiles. Yeshua refers to this material as "My commandments." The vast bulk of His teaching consisted of explicit Torah passages and Torah-based instruction. Moreover, since He was most likely speaking Hebrew to His Hebrew-speaking followers, He would have used the word "mitzvot," which we have translated "commandments." Mitzvot were part of the instructions of the Torah. In other words, it is not difficult to see that Yeshua would have been instructing His followers to teach the Torah (the teaching on God's righteousness) to those from among the Gentiles who would believe. This would have been perfectly consistent with the prophecy of Isaiah 56 which we examined above.

Introducing the Gentile to the Torah

The next important passage relating to our subject is Acts 15. To be sure, this is not an easy passage to interpret. It is, however, an important passage for us because it contains a record of how the Gentile believers were received by the early Jewish followers of Yeshua. There are several things we can learn from this passage about how Gentile believers may relate to the Torah.

The first point made by Acts 15 is that no one may follow Torah in order to achieve justification. Concerning this salvation, the leaders confirmed that "God made no distinction between us and them, for He purified their hearts by faith" (verse 9). Having stated this truth, however, the chapter tells us that the Jewish leadership definitely had the Torah in the forefront of their minds. In verses 19–21, we see the leaders concluding that the new Gentile believers had a very definite relationship to the Torah. There were several aspects to this relationship.

First, presumably to facilitate table fellowship between the Jewish and non-Jewish members of the Body of Messiah, the Jerusalem elders instructed the non-Jewish believers to follow the parts of the Torah which had to do with the dietary laws. This was important, because it was through sharing meals together that true fellowship and unity could be fostered between the once estranged cultures.

It is at this point that many otherwise careful commentators fall into a trap. They assume that the Jewish leadership was requiring the Gentiles to follow something similar to the famous "Noachide Laws"—a set of rules developed by the rabbis for Gentiles to follow in order to be considered righteous. It is true that the four requirements recorded in Acts 15 are very similar to these Noachide Laws. However, we disagree with most interpretations of the reason for these requirements.

Many teachers feel that since the rabbis required Gentiles to adhere to the Noachide Laws, the Jewish leadership here is simply following suit, albeit on a somewhat limited basis. That may be true. However, there is a second, more probable explanation: the Jewish elders in Jerusalem were doing all they could to demonstrate grace, patience, and kindness to the Torah-illiterate Gentile believers.

The Jewish believers had grown up with the Torah. Many had significant sections of it memorized. It was their life and breath, their joy and heartbeat (see Acts 21). But to the Gentiles the Torah was a strange book. Many had never even been exposed to it before Sha'ul and other faithful followers of Yeshua brought them the message of Messiah. The Jerusalem elders knew this. They also knew that the only existing body of teaching for believers, Jewish or Gentile, was the Torah. However, the elders could not demand that the Gentile believers follow the Torah with the same intensity that they did. Therefore, by delineating the four Torah-based instructions for table fellowship in Acts 15:19–20, the wise and loving elders were communicating to the Gentiles this message: "You are equal to us in the Body of Messiah. Our teachings are your teachings. But it will take you a while before you can understand the Holy Book, the Torah. Thus, for now, only learn what will best facilitate fellowship between you and your Jewish brothers and sisters. You will gradually learn more of what it means to walk with God as time goes by. We will send you qualified and trained Torah teachers."

We find a confirmation of this interpretation in verse 21. After the elders wrote the teachings in verses 19–20, they made this rather cryptic statement to the Gentiles: "For Moses has been preached in every city from the earliest times and is read in the synagogues on every Shabbat." What is the meaning of this comment? It seems to make very little sense— *unless* we understand it as the elders' encouragement of the Gentile believers to continue in their study of the Torah. And since Torah instruction was available in the local synagogue of almost every city in the diaspora, this would not have presented a problem! In other words, the Jewish elders were telling the Gentile believers that if they wanted to grow in their understanding of the Torah, they could learn how to do so— in the synagogue.

Moreover, because most Gentile believers would have been worshiping in the synagogues, the Jerusalem leadership knew that these new believers would be hearing the Torah each week. In their wisdom, they knew the reality of Yeshua's teaching that "the sheep know My voice and follow Me." The Torah is the voice of Yeshua, and these young lambs would hear and follow.

Thus Acts 15, far from downplaying the role of Torah in the life of non-Jewish believers, rather provides ample encouragement for them to pursue the Torah at their own pace.

Gentiles Grafted In

We have seen that Abraham, the father of our faith, "heard God's voice and guarded God's Torah." We also saw that the Torah itself made provision for the Gentiles to relate to it. Next we looked at Isaiah's magnificent prophecies to the Gentile remnant of believers concerning their relationship to Torah and Israel's covenant. After that, we learned that Yeshua instructed His followers to teach the Gentiles the Torah, as the elders of the young Jerusalem fellowship knew that the Gentile converts would hear and pursue it.

Now we come to one of the most important passages concerning the relationship between Gentile and Jewish believers in Yeshua. We are referring to Romans 11:11–21. To be sure, this passage does not speak about the Torah. However, it does teach that Gentile believers have a significant relationship with Israel. It is only a matter of reasoning that, since Gentile believers are closely connected to Israel, then they must also have a close connection to the Torah—just as Deuteronomy 4 implies.

In Romans 11:11–21, Shaul provides one of the most exciting truths in the Brit Chadasha for Gentile believers. Elsewhere he had described unbelieving Gentiles as those who were "uncircumcised, foreigners to the covenants of the promise, without hope, far away" (Ephesians 2:11–13), and pagan idol-worshipers (I Corinthians 12:2). In contrast, because of what Messiah Yeshua did for these countless numbers of non-Jewish people, they have now been brought near and "grafted in" to Israel.

There is some difference of opinion among the scholars about exactly into what the Gentiles are grafted. Some say that they, along with Jewish believers, are grafted in to Yeshua. But that does not do the passage or the context justice. Wilson states it best when he observes, "But this view confuses the expression 'root of Jesse'...or 'root of David'...with 'root of the olive tree.' The flow of the context supports the conclusion that the root represents the patriarchs: Abraham, Isaac, and Jacob, the faithful forefathers of the Jews."[15]

Thus, this passage is telling us that Gentile believers in Yeshua have a significant relationship with Israel through being grafted in. Again, let us permit Wilson to summarize this beautiful truth for us:

> Thus the Church, firmly planted in Hebraic soil, finds its true identity in connection with Israel. The Church is fed, sustained, and supported by that relationship.[16]

What then does it mean, in practical terms, for Gentiles to be "grafted in" to the olive tree of Israel? As stated elsewhere in this book, it does not mean that Gentile believers are now Jews. That, as we have stated, is a matter of physical descent. Rather, it is the fulfillment of Isaiah's prophecy: Gentiles can now benefit from the covenants, resulting in a living and active relationship with the Torah. Remember what Ephesians 2:11–13 says:

> Remember that formerly you who are Gentiles by birth...you were separate from Messiah, excluded from citizenship in Israel and foreigners and strangers to the covenants of the promise.... But now you have been brought near through the blood of Messiah.

The Gentile believers have not been grafted in to France, nor have they been brought near to China or Mexico. Rather, because of Messiah, they are "no longer foreigners and aliens, but fellow citizens with God's people and members of God's household...." They have been made part of the common-wealth of the children of Israel.

An Inheritance with Israel

Lest there be any doubt about the new relationship between Gentile believers and the covenanted children of Israel, let us turn to Ezekiel 47. Here the prophet looks far ahead of his own time, and even of our present age. He prophesies concerning the coming Messianic Age, when Yeshua will be seated on the throne of David in Jerusalem. This will also be the time, according to Ezekiel, when the final land inheritance is divided among the people of Israel.

However, we see in verses 21–23 that there will be others desiring to live among the people of Israel. These are Gentile believers. The Lord at that time will instruct Israel with the following word regarding the distribution of the inheritance:

> "You are to distribute this land among yourselves according to the tribes of Israel. You are to allot it as an inheritance for yourselves and for the aliens who have settled among you and who have children. You are to consider them as native-born Israelites; along with you they are to be allotted an inheritance among the tribes in Israel. In whatever tribe the alien settles, there you are to give him his inheritance," declares the Sovereign Lord.

Do you see what God is teaching here? He is instructing the Israelites regarding their relationship with those who have come to live among them. They are so grafted in that they are to be considered native-born Israelites, with full rights of inheritance. One thing this implies for our study is that if non-Jewish believers may be entitled a parcel of land among the people of Israel in the Messianic kingdom, surely they can be permitted to enjoy the blessings of the Torah among the people of Israel right now!

The Bride

We have indicated in this book that, among other things, the Torah serves as the ketubah, the sacred marriage document specifying the conditions for the divine marriage between God and Israel. This means that Israel is the bride of God, a fact quite adequately affirmed in the rest of the Tenach (see, for example, the prophecy of Hosea). Yet, as we read the Brit Chadasha, we learn that the "Church" is considered to be the bride of Messiah.

What is the situation here? Does God have two brides? Is He a polygamist? Of course not! Or is it possible that, as some have suggested, God divorced one bride, Israel, to marry another, the Church? That cannot be, either. Jeremiah speaks concerning this when he affirms God's everlasting covenant with the physical children of Israel in 31:35–37. Sha'ul of Tarsus also affirms the continual existence of the physical people of Israel in Romans 9–11.

The best solution to this problem is to assert that God has always had one bride, His chosen people. His bride has always been Israel, remnant Israel. All along, this has been enlarged to include those grafted in to Israel, the Gentile believers. Since, therefore, God has one bride, it would then follow that the same ketubah still defines this divine marriage: the Torah.

The Cycle of Worship

Finally, we need to ask one question: where are the commanded worship times that God gave to His people? We can look long and hard through the Brit Chadasha without finding a specified time of worship for the people of God. Yet all we need do is open to Leviticus 23, and a whole worship cycle is before us. This cycle contains seven or eight specified times when God's holy community gathers for precious worship before the Holy One. Most of these special appointed times (*mo'adim* in Hebrew) are occasions of great joy and praise. One day, Yom Kippur, is a more solemn occasion. In short, these are the times when Israel was called to remember what God did for them as a nation, both physically and spiritually. The cycle of the mo'adim was designed by God to proclaim in every generation, year by year, the Good News of the Messiah and His work of redemption in our lives (see also Hebrews 4:2). Accordingly, it should not surprise us that the Lord commanded these special days to be observed "throughout your generations wherever you live" (23:14, 21).

What about the non-Jewish members of God's family? Are they to be left out of the singing and the dancing, the celebrating of the Lord's redemptive work in their lives? Are they to be denied gathering for special meals, hearing the shofar sound, or living for a week in a special *succah*? Yet these are the specified times of worship taught in the Torah and which Yeshua celebrated with His *talmidim* (disciples).

The history of redemption and the worship of the Redeemer were clearly intended to be celebrated by all of God's people throughout the generations through the mo'adim. This includes the Gentile believers, as they are part of that same redemptive history. (For those unfamiliar with the mo'adim, we refer you to Chapter Three, "The Torah, a Way of Life," as an introduction to the subject.)

Summary

We have attempted in this section to present the biblical evidence supporting this thesis: that non-Jewish believers in Yeshua have a meaningful and significant relationship to the Torah of Moshe. Through this relationship, God Himself instructs His children to embrace the full revelation of His grace in their lives. That full revelation consists of the whole of Scripture, including the Torah.

Believing Israel in the first century was a mighty light to the nations. As a result, many from those nations came to faith and were "grafted in" to the holy community. The holy community is the Torah community. May the holy community of this present generation also become a light to the nations, bringing many into "the Way, the Truth and the Life"—Yeshua Himself! According to our understanding…is the Torah for me? Yes! For you? Are you grafted in? Then, yes! The Torah is for the holy community!

Chapter Five
Why Follow the Torah?

Why Follow the Torah?

In a sense, this chapter might be considered a continuation of Chapter Three, which dealt with the purposes for the Torah. However, the thrust here primarily concerns the motivations for following Torah, rather than its purposes per se. Hence, there are several reasons why the Torah is to be lived. We have not presented these in order of importance; they are meant to be considered equally. As we do so, a more complete picture should unfold.

Because God Tells Us To!

One word frequently used to describe much of the content of the Torah is the Hebrew *mitzvah*. This simply means "commandment." It is something God has told us to do. Don't be frightened by the concept, as if it is something only for the

Tenach. Although Jewish scholars are quick to assert that there are 613 commandments in the Torah, New Testament scholars have noted that there are over 1,000 such "commandments" in the Brit Chadasha! A commandment is a commandment. After all, what is the difference between celebrating Shavuot and choosing elders to govern your fellowship? Both are commanded.

Torah Gives Definition

What does it mean to be Jewish? As noted earlier in the book, the Torah is the only authoritative document which answers this question. Many Jewish traditions are purely cultural, but the Torah presents a required lifestyle of holiness that is cross-cultural. Whether from Morocco or Brooklyn, Jewish people are bound together by certain practices, such as circumcision and eating kosher, that are taught in the Torah. It is the Torah, then, that gives the descendants of Jacob their identity. Believing in Yeshua only makes that identity complete.

Because it is Who We Are!

Personally, we like this reason the most because it solves all of the problems for both Jewish and non-Jewish people. If we follow Torah only because it is commanded, it can easily turn into legalism. Let us enter by a different door altogether. Let us enter the arena of Torah through the door of our identity in Messiah, and see where it leads us.

The Scripture teaches us a critical truth. In bringing us to faith in Yeshua, God has made us into completely new people. We are new creations, with the Messiah living in us. Moreover, we are receivers of and participants in the Brit Chadasha. Jeremiah 31 teaches that God promises to write Torah *on our hearts* when He makes us new. Do not miss the full implications of that. Torah is written on our hearts! Among other things, this means that Torah is part of our basic makeup as believers in Yeshua. The new-creation man or woman, therefore, should only do what comes naturally to him or her. In this case, it means living out what is written in the Word—*all* of the Word.

The Mirror

Why do we follow Torah? Because it is who we are as new creations. When we read of the redeemed person as described by the precepts of Torah, we are, in reality, reading a description of who God has made us in the Messiah. Let us return again to the concept of the mirror image referred to in James 1:22–25. Here we learn the importance of being doers of the Word instead of listeners only. The illustration is of a person looking at himself in a mirror, but verse 25 describes that "mirror" as the Torah. (Though translated "law" in nearly every English translation, it is actually *Torah*.) He who does not do the Word is one who looks at his face in the Torah and immediately forgets what he looks like. In that state, therefore, he does not do the Word. But the person who sees himself in the mirror—the Torah—and remembers what he looks like, this is the one who does the Word. When we look into the mirror of the Torah, our reflection is that of a redeemed person as described therein. The individual teachings, in essence, describe what the redeemed one looks like. Because it is Yeshua who has made us new, made us the righteousness of God (II Corinthians 5:21), all that is left for us to do is to choose to walk in that new life—the righteous life of Yeshua—the life of Torah.

Therefore, we do not follow Torah as though it were merely a list of do's and don'ts. We follow it because it is written on our hearts. It is who we are as new creations. It comes naturally to us because God has made us into new people! But unless we know what our real spiritual identity is, we can't enter into the whole realm of our new life in Messiah that is available through the Torah.

Because Our Messiah Did It

Don't all believers want to do what the Lord did, and to be like Him? We are quick to practice letting His love flow out from us, and learning to worship and pray as He worshiped and prayed. Rightly so. But what about following the Torah as Yeshua did? His life was so characterized by Torah that even as late as the next generation of Jewish believers after Him, He was referred to as "The Torah." Even John 1 describes Yeshua as the Word, a reference to the Torah.

There is one more key to this point which will unlock its importance for us. The key is to remember that Yeshua is in us! We are new creations, with the Living Torah inside of us. This truth is so powerful that, when we think about it, the question we should be asking is not "Should we follow the Torah?" but "How do we come to know this 'treasure in jars of clay'?" (II Corinthians 4:7)

Because of What it Communicates to Unbelievers

This is our final and most emotional point. We are speaking here as Jewish people to other Jewish people, believers especially. But we are also making an appeal to non-Jewish believers, who need to be awakened to a major theological tragedy that has been perpetuated for the last 1,800 years.

The anti-Torah theology which so dominates the body of Messiah today, originally taught and practiced in the second century, arose from a distinct anti-Judaism propounded by some of the most influential scholars and leaders in the body of Messiah. And because many theologians in the Body today have swallowed the anti-Torah teachings of the Church fathers, the conclusions they continue to teach and publish naturally reflect the same bias. The believers of our era may not be as anti-Jewish as many of the Church fathers were; nevertheless, many have inherited their anti-Torah, anti-Jewish interpretations of the Brit Chadasha Scriptures.

Many today do not think for themselves, nor practice honest exegesis of the Brit Chadasha. If they did, they would conclude that the Brit Chadasha, in reality, is very Torah-positive and encourages a Torah lifestyle. And while it is no easy task to change beliefs which have been dearly held for over 1,800 years, change they must—if for no other reason than to be honest with the Bible.

But there *is* another reason. We need to ask some very serious questions. What does the prevailing anti-Torah theology say to the traditional Jewish world? How do they see us? What do they understand of our thinking? Moreover, Jewish believers, what is the message being conveyed to our families and Jewish friends by our attitude toward Torah?

Simply stated, we are communicating confusion and error to the very people through whom the Word of truth originally came. As a result, on the human level (that is, apart from the elective grace of God) there is very little motivation within the traditional Jewish world to hear the Good News. Rabbi Benjamin Blech is a prominent teacher at New York's prestigious Yeshiva University, a major educational institution for the Orthodox Jewish world. In his excellent textbook on basic Judaism, he makes this very poignant criticism of "Christianity" as he understands it:

> Christianity therefore rejected the law and gave a new interpretation to the covenant at Sinai. This is the crucial distinction between the Old Testament and the New. The Torah was assuredly given to the Jewish people at Mount Sinai, but its laws were no longer binding, according to Christianity. How could God have given directives that He Himself later saw fit to change?[17]

Blech is saying that by rejecting Torah we have, at best, confused the Jewish people in regard to God's revelation in the Scriptures. At worst, we have written them off as a people group. Inasmuch as the Church's anti-Torah bias led to the theological (and physical) persecution of the Jewish people, Christian rejection of the Torah has ultimately resulted in Jewish rejection of Yeshua. In short, for our people, the Good News has become nothing but the sad and bad news.

The Church's anti-Torah theology is a tragic flaw as concerns the Jewish people. Dr. Stern recognizes this when he says,

> I am certain that the lack of a correct, clear, and relatively complete Messianic Jewish or Gentile Christian theology of the Torah is not only a major impediment to Christians' understanding their own faith, but also the greatest barrier to Jewish people's receiving the Gospel. Most Christians have an overly simplistic understanding of what the Torah is all about; and second, that Christianity has almost nothing relevant to say to Jews about one of the three most important issues of their faith.[18]

Are We Listening?

Our goal in pursuit of Torah will be accomplished when each reader can sing Psalm 19:7–11 along with David. Many believers do sing this song, in reference to the whole Word of God. This is fine. Remember, though, that when David wrote these words, he was writing about the Torah.

> The Torah of the Lord is perfect, restoring the soul; the testimony of the Lord is sure, making wise the simple. The precepts of the Lord are right, rejoicing the heart; the commandment of the Lord is pure, enlightening the eyes. The fear of the Lord is clean,

enduring forever; the judgments of the Lord are true and righteous altogether. They are more desirable than gold, yes, than much fine gold; sweeter also than honey and the drippings of the honeycomb. Moreover, by them Your servant is warned; in keeping them there is great reward.

Chapter Six
Jewish
Misconceptions of the Torah

Jewish
Misconceptions of the Torah

Some years ago, there was a game show on television which consisted of a master of ceremonies, a panel of "experts" (well-known celebrities), and three contestants—one of whom was a special guest. It was the job of the other two contestants to assume the identity of the guest, while the panel members interrogated all three to find out who was telling the truth. When the questioning was over, the master of ceremonies called on each member of the panel to decide which contestant he or she believed. The host would then say, "Will the real 'John Doe' please stand up!" The panel members who had correctly discerned between the real person and the impostors rejoiced, and the audience applauded. Finally, we all knew who the real "John Doe" was.

The concluding chapters in this pursuit of Torah will be something like that game show. We will focus on some Torah deceivers which have developed over the centuries—fraudulent "torahs" which some have attempted to pass off as the true Torah. We will look at one such impostor from the Jewish camp in this chapter. In the next chapter we will examine one from the "Christian" camp. We want our readers, the "panel of experts," to decide which is the true Torah.

The Dual Torahs—an Explanation

Let us begin with the Jewish concept of the "dual Torah." In Judaism there are two Torahs. One is called the written Torah, *Torah sh'Bichtav* (תורה שבכתוב), and the other is referred to as the oral Torah, *Torah sh'be'al peh* (תורה שבעל פה). Both are essential concepts of traditional Judaism, both ancient and modern. It is important to note, however, that the concept of dual torahs is *not* derived from the plural use of the word "torah." Keeping in mind the fact that "torah" means "teaching" will help us understand that, when used in the plural in Hebrew, "torah" simply refers to a section containing multiple instructions about a given subject, and not to the dual torah concept.

Moshe is Fundamental

The primary authority in the life of a religious Jewish person is the Torah. (Although the Hebrew word *Torah* simply means "teaching" and can refer to any body of teaching, such as the whole Tenach and the rabbinical writings, we are using the term here as it is most commonly understood—to indicate the first five books of Scripture, Genesis through Deuteronomy.) Harvey Lutzke underscores the centrality of the Torah to the Jewish people when he writes,

> The Torah, quite simply, is the backbone of the Jewish people. It is the source, the root, the basis for all Jewish life, and it is the very foundation of Judaism.

The Torah is without parallel. From the Torah came
all subsequent Jewish works.[19]

Not only is the written Torah fundamental to Judaism, it
is also the foundational document for all who follow the Brit
Chadasha. We simply cannot have one without the other. The
Brit Chadasha is built upon the teachings of the Torah.

"We Need to Know More"

Having established this basic tenet of Judaism, we immediately encounter a problem—or at least, what *seems* like a
problem. The written Torah is so basic that the reader may
feel he needs more information in order to fulfill its commands as intended. For example, Leviticus commanded Israel to slaughter animals as sacrifices for sin. But the offerers
were not told in what manner this was to be accomplished.
How was the animal to be held? Where was the incision to be
made? What, if anything, was to be said before slaughter-
ing? These and many other details are absent from the written Torah.

This apparent information gap was filled, according to
the sages, by the oral Torah. According to its simplest definition, oral Torah is that which was spoken by God to Moshe on
Mount Sinai and which Moshe, in turn, spoke to the Israelites. Furthermore, sometime before he died, according to the
Mishnah, Moshe "transmitted it to Joshua, Joshua to the Elders, the Elders to the Prophets; and the Prophets transmitted it to the Men of the Great Assembly." This quotation is
from the Mishnah, tractate Pirke Avot 1:1, and is considered
an introductory passage to all of Avot, one of the most respected tractates in all of the Mishnah. According to R. Pinchas
Kehati, a modern Mishnaic scholar from Jerusalem:

> The purpose of this opening statement is to teach us
> that every word cited in this tractate, as indeed the

whole of the oral Torah, can in their systematic form be traced back through the Prophets to Moshe Rabbenu, the father of all prophets, who received the whole Torah—its laws, rules of inference and interpretations—from the Almighty Himself. [20]

The Explanations, Too?

Up until Kehati's comments, it was relatively easy to grasp both the need for, and the idea of, an oral Torah. It is conceivable that God spoke more to Moshe than what he actually wrote down; moreover, it is even conceivable that Moshe passed down much instruction verbally to Joshua, and so on. But Kehati speaks of more than just explanatory or additional instruction from God. He said that when Moshe received the written Torah, he also received "laws, rules of inference and interpretations from the Almighty Himself." This means, among other things, that the proper interpretations for each Torah passage were also given to Moshe in the oral Torah.

Kehati did not invent this concept. Indeed, it existed from ages past. But one of the most forthright clarifications of this comes from the Rambam (Rabbi Moshe ben Maimon), the great twelfth-century Sephardic sage. In the introduction to one of his greatest works, the *Mishneh Torah*, Rambam wrote,

> All of the commandments (mitzvot) that were given to Moshe on Mount Sinai were given with their meaning, as it is written: "And I give you the tablets of stone and the Torah and the mitzvah"; the "Torah" is the written law and the "mitzvah" is the oral law. Before his death Moshe wrote down all of the Torah. He gave one book to each of the tribes and one book was put in the Ark for all time....He did not write down the "mitzvah," which is the explanation of the Torah, but taught it to the elders and to Joshua and to all of Israel.[21]

Thus, it becomes clear that the oral Torah is much more than a few additional teachings, passed down verbally from God to Moshe and thence to the great sages. In addition to these verbal teachings, it is claimed that God gave Moshe the understanding and correct interpretation of all of Torah. This, too, was passed on by word of mouth.

The Waters Get Very Muddy

There is yet a third part to the total concept of oral Torah. The teachings in the oral Torah were great for Moshe's generation, but what about the specific needs of subsequent generations? The rabbis answer this question by explaining that the written Torah gives each generation the authority to make rulings which are binding for that generation. The passage cited in support of this idea is Deuteronomy 17:8–13. Here, claim the rabbis, the written Torah grants the sages in each generation the power to make authoritative and binding halachic decisions. These rulings are also considered oral Torah.

Rabbi Simcha Cohen elucidates this idea when he writes, "In addition, since ours is a living law, binding on a Jew in whatever society he lives, the law must be clearly understood in the light of changing civilizations and different societies."[22] Cohen further illustrates this idea by citing Rambam, who decided to "update" the oral Torah for *his* generation.

Rambam states that he studied all the important and available writings—both Talmuds, the midrashim, the Tosefta, and others—in order "to learn from them what is forbidden and what is permitted, and other laws of the Torah."[23] As a result, the Rambam made his own compilation of the oral Torah "so that there will be one complete oral law, comprehensible to everyone without need for questioning or dissection."[24]

After the Rambam, R. Joseph Caro completed his update in the sixteenth century in the form of *Shulchan Aruch*.

Consequently, others following him did the same, such as the Chafetz Chaim in the twentieth century in his *Mishnah Brura*.

Fixed and Fluid

Thus, the oral Torah is basically comprised of three different components. It was eventually written down in the form of the *Mishnah* by R. Yehudah haNasi (Rabbi Judah the Prince, or "the Rabbi" in the Talmud) around the year 200 CE. He saw a need to make the oral Torah somewhat standard for the diverse and dispersed Jewish community. Thus, the oral Torah is, on the one hand, a fixed entity. However, because it was intended to meet the needs of each generation, it is also a fluid entity. Hence, Rabbi Cohen asserts that Rabbi Yehudah's Mishnah "was appropriate only for his generation."[25] Hence, the next generations of sages, called the *Amoraim*, produced the *Gemarah*. This commentary on the Mishnah was combined with it to produce the *Talmud*. The Talmud, then, is the most authoritative collection of oral Torah.

When we say that the oral Torah is fluid, we mean that each generation must study, know, and use the previous generation's oral Torah to formulate its halachic policies. At no point could a new oral Torah contradict an older one. What was binding for the Mishnah generation is also binding for us today.

Bearing in mind that this is a brief explanation of a very complex concept, let us now see if this oral Torah is the *true* Torah, or if we have an impostor here.

An Analysis

What are we to make of the concept of oral Torah? First, let us say that part of the concept does seem to make sense. As we have mentioned, Moshe may indeed have taught Israel more than he wrote down. One question which can be posed, however, is how accurately all of this information was passed on by scores of mouths over a period of hundreds of years. Moreover, does the written Torah actually teach that there was an oral Torah, as the rabbis insist? Finally, how much authority should we give to the body of literature known as the oral Torah?

The Torah itself hints against a divinely inspired oral tradition. One example is God's instruction in Deuteronomy 17:14–20 as to how a king of Israel must conduct himself while in office. God specifically told him to make a copy of the Torah for himself. Notice that the king was not directed to make a copy of a body of oral tradition and conduct his office from that. Rather, it was the written word that was to be his rule and authority. True, the king may have relied on traditional oral instruction, but if this was divinely inspired, one would expect God to have commanded him to conduct his kingship by that. God, however, gave no such instruction. The only authoritative guide for the kings of Israel was the written Torah.

The Torah which Hilkiah found and Josiah obeyed was not the so-called oral Torah. Rather, it was the written Word of God, which worked a deep, spiritual change among the people. This is not to say that all man-made traditions are wrong. However, two things are certain. First, if there was an *authoritative* oral tradition in existence in Josiah's day, there is no indication of it in the Scriptures; and second, it was the written Torah which God used to work spiritual reform among His people—not a body of oral laws.

The Holy One was careful to ensure that all necessary and binding revelation was written down and preserved accurately. If the so-called oral Torah were just as binding, it would seem natural and reasonable that it too would have been inscribed by Moshe. However, the biblical evidence, especially in the Prophets and the Writings, strongly mitigates against it.

Challenging the Rambam

Earlier in this study we cited Rambam's rationale for the oral Torah. He makes a distinction between Torah and mitzvot, saying that "the Torah" refers to the written Torah, while the oral Torah is comprised of the mitzvot.

This explanation seems reasonable on the surface. However, the Scriptures present a serious challenge to its accuracy. Consider the passage in which Joshua leads the people of Israel in a covenant renewal ceremony on Mount Gerizim and Mount Ebal. When the service was over, Joshua "read all the words of the Torah, the blessing and the curse, according to all that is written in the book of the Torah." The person writing this account, apparently Joshua, provides his own important commentary on the event in verse 35: "There was not a word of all that Moshe had commanded which Joshua did not read before all the assembly." (Joshua 8:31–35)

Verse 35 provides us with two pieces of information which are valuable for our analysis of oral Torah. First, it says that all that Moshe commanded was written and then read. Second, this includes the mitzvot! (The word "mitzvot" also appears many times in the written Torah.) The Hebrew word translated "commanded" is from the word *tzaveh* (צוה), the word from which we get "mitzvot." What Joshua was saying is that everything Moshe had spoken was written and read—including the mitzvot!

Let us go to one last passage from the Book of Joshua. This time we will examine 23:6–8. Here, the Lord Himself is encouraging Joshua to follow Him and His Word. In doing so, He writes,

> Be very firm, then, to keep and do all that is written in the book of the Torah of Moshe, so that you may not turn aside from it to the right hand or to the left, in order that you may not associate with these

nations, these which remain among you, or mention the name of their gods, or make anyone swear by them, or serve them, or bow down to them. But you are to cling to the Lord your God, as you have done to this day.

If an oral Torah existed, why did the Lord not command Joshua to cling to it as well as to "all that is written in the book of the Torah of Moshe?" Could it be that God really did give instruction which Moshe did not inscribe, but which He *did not intend* to be passed from generation to generation? We would like to submit that this is exactly what happened. Each generation was to follow the written Torah under the direction of the Spirit of God, and not with a fixed, established interpretation called oral Torah.

Justified Interpretations?

The sages also claim that the oral Torah helps us to understand the written Torah by providing the authoritative interpretations of the written Torah. Rabbi Cohen provides a vivid example. He relates the account of the secret removal of Rabbi Yochanan ben Zakkai from Jerusalem during the Roman siege led by Vespasian. Rabbi ben Zakkai saw the handwriting on the wall, so to speak, concerning the downfall of Jerusalem, and felt he should do all he could to help preserve Judaism. But because of the policies of the Zealots, Jews were not permitted to leave the city unless they were going to bury someone. This is exactly how he escaped—his followers carried him out in a coffin!

When he got to the Roman lines, the rabbi found a way to convince the general to let him through: he pronounced a prophecy concerning Vespasian's immediate future. In a short time, he said, Vespasian would become the new Emperor. (This actually came to pass while ben Zakkai was still being held by the Romans.) But he worded the prophecy in very cryptic terms. Ben Zakkai told him, "You will be King, because if you are not, Jerusalem will not be yours, as it is written, 'and the Lebanon will fall to a mighty one' [Isaiah 10:34], and there is no mighty one but a King."

Ben Zakkai cited Isaiah 10:34, and connected "Lebanon" with Jerusalem and the Temple Mount. By making this connection, he revealed his allegorical method of Torah interpretation, using an existing interpretation of Deuteronomy 3:25 found in the oral Torah. This use of the oral Torah in interpreting the written reveals "how the sages penetrated the written with the help of the oral tradition."[26] This example illustrates for us the relationship of the oral Torah to the written. The key phrase in this example is the last statement by Rabbi Cohen, *"Rabbi Yochanan's words reveal how the sages penetrated the written with the help of the oral tradition."* (italics ours)

However, does the oral tradition really help us to penetrate the written Scripture consistently and accurately? Take a closer look at Deuteronomy 3:25. Do we have any hermeneutical permission from the context to understand the word "Lebanon" as anything other than the literal geographical location just north of the land of Israel? By what authority do the ancient sages make such fanciful interpretations of Scripture, and call it oral Torah?

When a sage gave an interpretation of a Scriptural passage by following a series of qualifications, it was considered authoritative and therefore part of the oral Torah—whether or not it fit the context or plain meaning of the words! As we have already learned from Rabbi Cohen, the ancient rabbis— and modern ones—derive practices and understandings from Torah passages that do not seem to have any direct relation to the subject under discussion. Is this an honest and just way to handle God's precious words?

Yeshua challenged such erroneous interpretations of the written Torah in Matthew 5–7. Here Yeshua was discussing some Torah issues. Over and against the established oral tradition of His day, He provided the original, God-intended meaning of the passages under question. Every time we see the formula, "You have heard that it was said…but I say unto you," Yeshua is debunking an interpretation of the Torah based on a so-called oral Torah.

Yeshua and the Oral Torah—the Second Temple Period

According to Pirke Avot 1:1, the oral Torah was passed on to the generations after Moshe, including those of the late Second Temple period. In fact, Avot itself contains many quotations from distinguished sages who lived during that period. This, of course, was the age in which Yeshua lived and taught. "Jesus lived in a Jewish world," according to Dr. David Flusser, professor emeritus at Jerusalem's Hebrew University, "which was flourishing within the framework of the written law (the Bible) and the oral law (what later became the Talmud)."[27]

Flusser contends that Yeshua was in the thick of that world's religious conflicts. According to a growing consensus of modern scholars of the Brit Chadasha, Yeshua lived as an observant Jewish man, debating with many prominent rabbis of his day over issues related to both the written and oral Torahs. "Jesus was scrupulous in keeping the Jewish commandments," says Flusser. The question is, what was His relationship to the oral Torah?

Not His Authority

At least two things can be said about Messiah and the oral Torah. The first is that not only was He familiar with it, but in certain respects He followed it. In Yeshua's day, there were two schools of Pharisaism, the School of Shammai and the School of Hillel, representing two distinct understandings of oral Torah. (Shammai and Hillel were very influential rabbis of a generation just before Yeshua.) According to Flusser,

> When we examine Jesus' position on matters of Jewish law, it appears that on some things he accepted the view of the more stringent authorities—the School of Shammai—and on the others, especially on matters of ideology, he was closer to the School of Hillel, whose motto was, "Thou shalt love thy neighbor as thyself." These views become evident when we examine Jesus' teachings and compare them to the other rabbinical teaching of his day.[28]

Apparently Yeshua agreed with some interpretations of the written Torah which the oral Torah provided. However, accepting some teachings of oral Torah is far different than accepting its *divine origin*. Nor does it mean that He accepted or agreed with its authority.

Man's Laws over God's Torah

Let us look at one example which provides a clue as to Yeshua's true attitude toward the oral Torah. In Mark 7:1–8, Yeshua discusses with some other Pharisees the issue of ritual hand washing before a meal. Yeshua's disciples did not follow the teaching of this group of Pharisees, who took Him to task for it. Verse 3 explains the Pharisees' custom: "For the Pharisees and all the Jews do not eat unless they carefully wash their hands, thus observing the traditions of the elders...."

The final phrase, "observing the traditions of the elders," was conventionally used to denote the oral Torah. Yeshua was being reproved for failing to submit to the authority of oral Torah as observed by this group of Pharisees.

Yeshua gave His reasoning and His intended teaching, and then uttered these crucial words in verses 7–8:

Rightly did Isaiah prophesy of you hypocrites, as it is written, "This people honors Me with their lips, but their heart is far away from Me. But in vain do they worship Me, teaching as doctrines the precepts of men. Neglecting the commandment of God, you hold to the tradition of men."

This was spoken as a rebuke to those who had criticized Him for breaking the oral Torah. It strikes at the very heart of the issue of written versus oral Torah. He tells them, as He would on other occasions, *"Neglecting the commandment of God, you hold to the tradition of men."* Yeshua found no problem with the teachings of the oral Torah when they provided insights or explanations that were true and accurate to the written Torah. However, there were times when the oral Torah was granted authority equal to—and even superseding—that of the written.[29] When this happened, Yeshua proclaimed the oral Torah to be merely the teachings of men, not of God! In issuing such a rebuke, He was also stating that He did not consider the oral Torah to be authoritative for the man of God, the man of Torah.

The Value of the Oral Torah

We do not accept the authority of the body of Jewish literature known as the oral Torah, nor do we view it as the inspired Word of God. However, there can be tremendous value in reading and studying rabbinic literature. In fact, even Yeshua followed some rabbinic traditions.

Dr. David Friedman is a Messianic Jewish scholar living in Israel. An expert on the Second Temple period, Dr. Friedman points out that the early rabbinic literature, such as the Mishnah and Talmud, can be invaluable in helping us to understand the historical and religious background of the Brit Chadasha. Friedman states,

As the Jewish talmudic scholar Shmuel Safrai of Hebrew University has pointed out, rabbinic literature, and the Talmud in particular, is by far our best source for understanding the structure, priestly function, sacrificial methods, and festival ceremonies of the Second Temple. Since Yeshua lived in this world, since He carried out His teachings at the Temple, and since He sacrificed and attended festival ceremonies there, it is worthwhile to be familiar with the Talmud's description of these areas.[30]

Rabbinic Text	Possible Background Purpose
Mishnah Sanhedrin	Justice and Court Systems of the Second Temple Period
Mishnah Yadayim	Pharisaic Purity Ideas of Second Temple Period
Mishnah Succot	Pharisaic Laws and Customs
Mishnah Yoma	Second Temple Yom Kippur Rituals
Dead Sea Scrolls	Understanding Dead Sea Sect Views on Purity, Serving God, Messiah, and Community
Pirke Avot	Rabbinic Worldview of Yeshua's Time
Book of Maccabees	History of Israel 150–100 Years Before Yeshua, Start of Chanukah Holiday
Midot	Temple Structure
Tamid	Second Temple Daily Ritual
Shekalim	Second Temple Taxation System

Chart: endnote 31

In addition to aiding our understanding of the Brit Chadasha, the oral Torah can also serve to heighten the appreciation of the Church for the efforts that Jewish people have made throughout history to protect, preserve, spread, and interpret the Scriptures. While we may disagree with some rabbinic interpretations, there are nevertheless other areas in which the oral Torah has been extremely helpful in its insights into the Torah and other parts of the Tenach.

Moreover, the rabbinic writings have been extremely beneficial in teaching us how to follow many commandments of the Torah. For example: how do we affix a mezuzah on the door? How do we celebrate Pesach? How do we properly slaughter a kosher animal for food? The oral Torah provides many excellent suggestions for following these and other teachings of the written Torah. And while we do not consider the rabbis' instructions to be the only way to do these things, they nevertheless can prove very instructive. Furthermore, as we follow the rabbinic practices—so long as they do not contradict either the Tenach or the Brit Chadasha—we are standing in solidarity with our people.

Finally, reading and studying the oral Torah lends tremendous insight into the minds of the great Jewish sages. As we learn what they thought, what they felt, and how they looked at life, we will be better able to appreciate the Jewish sensibility throughout the ages. It is hoped that this would help to curb the anti-Semitism which has run rampant through much of the Church's history.

It is now time for you, the members of our "panel," to render an opinion. Is the oral Torah a real, genuine Torah from the Holy One, equal to the written Torah in its power to transform a soul and in its spiritual authority? Does the written Torah permit us to assume an oral Torah, given by God to Moshe but authoritative for every generation? Or are we to depend on the leading and teaching of the Spirit of God to apply Torah's precepts to our generation?

Spiritual Authority

At stake here, among other things, is the issue of spiritual authority. Are we to obey God's teachings as written, or are we required to obey the megalith of minute details outlined by the rabbis in the oral Torah?

Some believe that the oral Torah is a fixed entity. We must do, they say, only what the rabbis tell us we are allowed to do, as expressed both in the Talmud and in their offices today. But do their laws carry true spiritual authority, equal to the "Thus says the Lord" of the Tenach?

For the believer, the key issue is to live the Torah as God actually gave it. The first saying in Pirke Avot provides a sad clue to the rabbinical idea behind oral Torah. After informing us of the genealogy of the oral Torah, the writer of this Mishnah exhorts us to "make a fence for the Torah." It must be said that the intentions behind this idea were beyond reproach. The sages, in search of a way to prevent their people from breaking the written Torah, decided to construct a fence around it. As Kehati writes, "The Torah charges the Rabbinical Courts to devise provisions, decrees, and restrictions which will prevent a person from violating a law of the Torah."[32]

This system of prevention, however, as admirable as it may seem, possesses an inherent flaw. What actually happens in this process is that the true Torah (God's teaching in regard to His righteousness) is changed into man-made laws which, not being the words of life, cannot bring forth life. Rabbi Sha'ul of Tarsus, himself thoroughly trained in the oral Torah, aptly says concerning the Torah teachers of his day: Since they did not know the righteousness that comes from God, they seek to establish their own; and in so doing, they do not submit to God's righteousness. (Romans 10:1–8, our paraphrase)

"Law" versus Torah

God has revealed His mind, heart, and righteousness in the written Torah. The original writers recorded what He spoke to them with 100% accuracy. No one has the right to make even one change in this written revelation. If a halacha is developed which does not match the Torah teaching exactly as written, it ceases to be consistent with the words of life, and hence cannot bring forth the life of Messiah in the believer.

With this thought in mind, return to Figure 1 on page 29. Notice a line inside the border of Torah and a line outside the border. Any halacha which "hits the mark," or at least lands inside it, is life-giving Torah. Any and all halacha landing *outside* the mark, however, is not true Torah. The words of Torah are the "protective guards" which God Himself set in place for His children. Just as Abraham protected God's protective guards, then, so must we be found faithful to do the same. (Genesis 26:5 [see page 29])

When God gave the Torah, He also instructed us in how to view it. He specifically advised us that its commandments were not impossible to obey. Because this is true, and knowing the tendency of man in his flesh, God was warning us not to develop a mentality that says, "You must obey exactly as the 'experts' say it must be obeyed, because their explanation is binding for their generation."

Oral Torah consists of an interpretation of the written Torah and, according to the rabbis, an authoritative halacha based on that interpretation. Our loving Father knew what men would try to do to the written Torah, perverting it into an oral one. He knew that the oral Torah experts would pronounce the believer unable to understand the Torah without their help. Knowing this tendency in people, the Lord wrote a safeguard for us in Deuteronomy 30:11–14. He said,

For this commandment which I command you today is not too difficult for you, nor is it out of reach. It is not in heaven, that you should say, "Who will go up to heaven for us to get it for us and make us hear it, that we may observe it?" Nor is it beyond the sea, that you should say, "Who will cross the sea for us to get it for us and make us hear it, that we may observe it?" But the word is very near you, in your mouth and in your heart, that you may observe it.[33]

Rabbi Sha'ul exhorts Messianic believers to this effect in Romans 10. Here, quoting Deuteronomy 30:11–14, he explains how one who has God's righteousness views the Torah. He says, "But the righteousness based on faith speaks thus, 'Do not say in your heart, "Who will ascend into heaven?"'...or "Who will descend into the abyss?"'" Why does the righteousness based on faith speak in this way? Because the person with God's righteousness *knows* what His original instructions to us were and still are. They are very clear.

Sha'ul was well versed in the oral Torah. He knew its pitfalls. He also knew that those who fostered the oral Torah were, in reality, turning the Torah into "law." This law did not reflect the righteousness of God; rather, it was the codification of man's righteousness. But Sha'ul said that one who has God's righteousness does not need to look high or low for its proper interpretation or application. Instead, God's Torah is always accessible to him.

Romans 10:2 teaches us that a person can be zealous for God with a zeal not based on knowledge. Does zealousness confirm or establish truth? According to Sha'ul's teaching in Romans 10, such a zealot merely establishes his own righteousness, while ignoring God's righteousness as expressed in the written Scriptures.

It is important to bear in mind that Judaism, as known by some of its most prominent scholars, does not consider itself a legalistic religion. Indeed, some of its most ardent spokesmen would cringe at the idea. The eminent Jewish New Testament scholar Pinchas Lapide affirms this idea when he says, "The rabbinate has never considered the Torah as a way of salvation to God...[rather we] regard salvation as God's exclusive prerogative, so that we Jews are the advocates of 'pure grace.'"[34]

That may be true, at least in theory. But most of the Jewish world has either lost sight of that biblical understanding, or practiced their faith in such a way as to convey that the purpose of their obedience to Torah is to earn a place in the world to come. Thus, we also concur with Bean when he says, "In spite of this [Judaism's purported emphasis on grace], one of Paul's main problems was the teachings of Judaizers, who insisted that both Jewish and Gentile believers must obey the letter of the Law."[35]

Being well versed in the traditional rabbinic thinking of his day, therefore, Sha'ul deemed it essential to counteract any semblance of legalism both within and without the believing community. Thus his characterization of Judaism in Romans 10 was not only accurate, but central to his point: zeal and sincerity notwithstanding, works-based righteousness has no place in God's kingdom.

Has the true Torah been distorted by the assignment of divine authority to the oral Torah, and by legalistic obedience to the written? Members of the panel, render your decisions. When the master of ceremonies intones, "Will the true Torah please stand up," will the oral Torah arise—or another?

Chapter Seven
Christian
Misconceptions of the Torah

Christian
Misconceptions of the Torah

In Chapter Six, we looked at a Jewish misconception of God's Torah. Now we will examine a Christian misconception of the Torah. We will see historically how some attempted to discourage believers from following the Torah in two different ways: first, by suggesting that the Torah had been done away with; and second, by changing the mental (and verbal) concepts of Torah into a concept called "law."

Let us look briefly at Church history. Here we can learn much about what motivated some of the ancient Church leaders to discourage believers from following the Torah. Then, after having established the necessary historical foundation, we will examine some selected passages from the Brit Chadasha which are often used to teach against Torah observance.

A Bitter History Lesson

Have you ever tried to turn back 1,800 years of history? In essence, if we are to develop and teach a biblically accurate theology of the Torah, that is precisely what we must do.

Christian misunderstanding of the Torah is a complex issue. It stems from a gross misinterpretation of several biblical passages, mostly in the writings of Sha'ul of Tarsus. But this contemporary misinterpretation is bolstered by approximately 1,800 years of anti-Jewish rhetoric from some of the Church's so-called finest exegetes—the Church fathers.

I (Ariel) first studied Church history over twenty years ago, both in Bible college and in seminary. My professors were truly gifted, godly men, teaching excellent courses from textbooks which are still used in many evangelical theological schools today. Looking back, however, I wonder, "Why were we not taught about the Jewish believers? Why was so little mentioned about the relationship between the Church and the Jewish people? Why do these textbooks present such a rosy picture of the Church fathers, when some of them were among the most anti-Jewish people who have ever lived?"

We do not know the full answer to these questions. Perhaps, because there were so few Jewish believers twenty years ago, there was simply little or no interest in these subjects. But whatever the reason, the fact remains that these curricula not only omitted some of the most significant events in the lives of the early believers—the majority of whom were Jewish—but actually covered up the real stories behind many of the theological decisions of the Church fathers and councils.

Whether or not these omissions were perpetrated consciously, the result is that many passages in the Brit Chadasha have been grossly misinterpreted, with an anti-Torah bias, throughout the centuries. Let us look at some of the history of the early Church in order to see how this occurred.

Acts 21: The Key

Our survey of ancient Church history must begin with a brief look, again, at Acts 21. We need to return to it one last time because of its significance to Church history. There are two aspects of this passage that are crucial for our purposes here: the chronology and the hermeneutical principle which the passage inadvertently establishes.

Many evangelical Bible teachers assert that we can obtain very little theology from the Book of Acts because, they say, it is a transitional book. Indeed, in many ways it is. Consider Luke's description of the outreach of Yeshua's followers as it shifted from a Jewish audience to one that was predominantly Gentile. One reason Acts was written was to show how the Church first acquired so many believers from a Gentile background.

If described in these or similar terms, we can accept the labeling of Acts as a transitional book. But many scholars go beyond the scope of history and assert a theological transition. In explaining why the focus of attention in Acts is on Sha'ul of Tarsus, evangelical mainstay Merrill C. Tenney says this:

> Since Paul was the leader of the Gentile mission, he deserved primary attention, and the explanation of the *transition* from Jew to Gentile, *from law to grace*, and from Palestine to the empire did not call for a comprehensive survey of all that took place in the missionary growth of the Christian church. For Luke's purpose the presentation of this one phase was sufficient.[36] (Italics ours)

The source for this quotation is the revised edition of Tenney's *New Testament Survey*, one of the standard textbooks in many Bible colleges for New Testament introduction or survey courses.

Notice how Tenney describes the transition in Acts. For him, and many others like him, it was not merely a transition from a predominantly Jewish body of Messiah to a predominantly Gentile one. Rather, it was also a transition "from law to grace." Acts 21 makes such a conclusion untenable. If there had been such a theological transition intended by God, then we would expect to see fewer and fewer believers following the Torah. Instead, Acts 21 tells us that some thirty years after Yeshua sent His students around the world to tell others of His grace, there grew such a strong Jewish congregation in Jerusalem that it was noted "how many thousands there are among the Jews of those who have believed, and they are all zealous for the Torah" (verse 20).

Notice several details about this verse. First, the number of people involved. Most English translations read "thousands." However, the Greek text (myriads) should be translated "*tens* of thousands." It is extremely difficult to be precise on how large the city of Jerusalem was just before its fall in 70 CE. The estimates range from 80,000 to 400,000.[37] No matter what the size, the text in Acts presents the fact that there were "many tens of thousands" of Jewish believers (apparently over 30,000) in Jerusalem at that time. This number constituted a significant percentage of the population.

In addition, this large number of Jewish believers were "all zealous for the Torah." If it's true that God actually designed a theological transition from "law to grace," then someone should have told these hordes of Messianic zealots! After all, thirty years is thirty years, a long enough time to show signs of such a transition. On the other hand, could it be they understood that the Torah was a written expression of God's grace, realized through acceptance of the Messiah Yeshua's sacrificial atonement?

Sha'ul's Golden Moment

So much for the chronological importance of this passage. What can it tell us about hermeneutics? Plenty!

By the time the events recorded in Acts 21 took place, Sha'ul's epistles to the Galatians and Romans were history, according to Tenney. It is precisely these two epistles which have been used by many a Bible scholar to "prove" that the Torah has been declared obsolete.

An accurate interpretation of Acts 21 should put an end to such thinking. To be sure, because Sha'ul had written Galatians and Romans by that time, his views regarding the Torah began to be misunderstood—so much so, that the leaders of the Jerusalem believers challenged him concerning his views (verses 17–26). It was rumored, they said, that he was "teaching all of the Jews among the Gentiles to forsake Moshe, telling them not to circumcise their children nor to walk according to the customs" (verse 21). The elders then demanded that Sha'ul either acknowledge the truth of the charges against him, or prove them false.

Here was a golden theological opportunity for Sha'ul of Tarsus. His next move *should* have constituted the defining moment for the Church in regard to the proper attitude of the believer toward the Torah. However, while what Sha'ul chose to do was absolutely clear in the text and to all who witnessed his actions, it certainly was not heeded by the rest of the Church, to judge by the centuries of anti-Torah rhetoric that followed! For the record, let it be pointedly stated (as we did earlier in this book): Sha'ul chose to uphold the Torah of Moshe. He chose to follow it and to encourage—even teach—other believers in Yeshua to make it their lifestyle. Acts 21:23–26 makes this clear in no uncertain terms.

If Sha'ul—or any other teacher—is to be trusted and his teaching followed, then it goes without saying that the conduct of his life must live up to the moral and ethical standards of his teaching. Sha'ul would not say one thing while doing the opposite. He would not write in Galatians and Romans, or any other of his letters, instructions to abandon or disregard the Torah if he himself used it as the basis for his lifestyle—that would be unthinkable!

We see, therefore, that Acts 21 must become part of our hermeneutics. On the surface, Sha'ul's writings may seem to indicate that the Torah should be done away with or disregarded by believers; however, Acts 21 requires us to dismiss that interpretation as invalid. The principles of biblical hermeneutics dictate that we use our knowledge of Sha'ul's conduct in Acts 21 to help us interpret his writings.

The Mess that Followed

The events related in Acts 21 took place sometime in the early to mid-sixties CE. From that time until after the Bar Kochba war—the Second Jewish Revolt, ending in 135 CE—many complicated events happened in both Church and Jewish history. Quite often, what happened to one affected the other. This was especially the case after the Second Jewish Revolt.

By the year 135 CE, the Church's population was predominantly Gentile, although a large and strong Jewish believing community still existed. By this time, however, there was a significant separation between the Church and the Synagogue. One principal reason for this was the unwillingness of many non-Jewish believers to suffer the wrath of imperial Rome that had come upon their nationalistic Messianic Jewish brethren.

Jewish believers had been fully willing to participate in the Bar Kochba rebellion (132–135 CE) until Rabbi Akiva declared him to be the Messiah. At that point they could no longer fight alongside their Jewish countrymen. Yet to Rome they were still Jewish. Moreover, their sentiments were for their own homeland, as opposed to Rome. Thus, the Jewish believers suffered as much as the rest of the Jewish people after Bar Kochba's failed revolution. The non-Jewish element in the Church, however, saw no reason to identify with this Jewish nationalism. Hence, they sought various means to demonstrate to Rome that they were not a Jewish sect, as Rome had previously assumed them to be.

Historian Hugh Schonfield states the issue clearly:

> The political crisis in Jewish affairs engendered among the Churches of the Empire a coldness and aloofness towards the Jewish Christians, which, after the Second Jewish Revolt in the reign of Hadrian, led to almost complete separation. The Roman Christians could not be expected to sympathize with the national aspirations of the Nazarenes. For them the destruction of Jerusalem and the cessation of the Temple services meant the end of the law. It came to them as a happy release from the incubus of Judaism and left them free to develop a Christian philosophy of their own better suited to the Gentile temperament.[38]

From the Jewish Side

Meanwhile, there were other factors contributing to the separation between the Jewish and non-Jewish elements, both inside and outside the Church. Rabbinic Judaism, in an attempt to define itself after the fall of the Temple in 70 CE, also caused the believers in Yeshua to feel uncomfortable in their community. It was during this time that the famous "benediction" against the "*minim*," or heretics, became a fixture in many synagogues as the *Amidah* was prayed.[39] Again, the precise history of this is vague, but essentially the words against the heretics amounted to a curse pronounced against believers in Yeshua, particularly Jewish believers. Moreover, the non-Jewish believers also took offense at this, provoking further animosity between them.

A good example of how the non-Jewish element of the Church received such rabbinic practices is found in the writings of Justin Martyr, a Church leader who lived circa 100–165 CE. In his famous *Dialogue with Trypho* (a Jewish man), Dialogues 16 and 96, he writes:

> "To the utmost of your power you dishonor and curse in your synagogues all those who believe in Christ....In your synagogues you curse too those who through them have become Christians, and the Gentiles put into effect your curse by killing all those who merely admit that they are Christians."

The Irreparable Rift

The Church's desire to convince Rome of their non-Jewishness was one thing. But the way they chose to do it was quite another, and it has left a permanent black mark on the history of biblical interpretation and the relationship between Church and Synagogue ever since. Already quite anti-Jewish in their teachings, and fueled by a growing anti-Semitic sentiment as well as the flamboyant rhetoric of its leaders, the Church began in the mid-second century to issue a series of anti-Jewish laws, some of which are still esteemed today.

At the core of this preaching was a severe attack against the Torah and its teachings. In this example from the *Epistle of Barnabas*, dating from between 130–138 CE, we see that there apparently were many believers who were sympathetic to Jewish people, perhaps even living Torah-centered lifestyles themselves. Against such, *Barnabas* (not to be confused with the Barnabas found in Acts, though the epistle would have us believe them to be one and the same) writes:

> Take heed to yourselves and be not like some, piling
> up your sins and saying that the covenant is theirs
> as well as ours. It is ours, but they lost it completely
> just after Moses received it.... (*Epistle* 4:6–7)

Writing shortly after this epistle, Justin Martyr (quoted above) declares not only that the covenant no longer belongs to the Jewish people, but also that the signs of both the Abrahamic and Mosaic covenants—circumcision and Shabbat respectively—have no further validity.

> We, too, would observe your circumcision of the flesh,
> your Sabbath days, and in a word all your festivals,
> if we were not aware of the reason why they were
> imposed upon you, namely, because of your sins and
> your hardness of heart. (*Dialogue* 18, 2)

Bacchiocchi concludes from such statements that the adoption of Sunday as the Christian day of worship went hand in hand with the anti-Jewish and anti-Torah teaching which had begun to proliferate: "What better way to evidence the Christians' distinction from the Jews than by adopting a different day of worship?" Moreover, by rejecting the Torah and replacing it with pagan ideas, such as venerating the day of the Sun, people like Martyr may also have been attempting to "make the Emperor aware that Christians were not Jewish rebels but obedient citizens...the Romans already at that time venerated the day of the Sun...and repeated reference to such a day could well represent a calculated effort to draw the Christians closer to the Roman customs than to those of the Jews."[40]

And the Beat Goes On

Thus, the anti-Torah attitudes of the early Church began as an effort both to make the Good News palatable to the pagans and to convince the imperial government of Rome that they were not Jews, thereby skirting any anti-Jewish enmity on the part of the government. Once the door was opened for anti-Torah interpretation in a predominantly non-Jewish Church, it became increasingly difficult to shut. Many of the most well-known and respected Church leaders walked through that door, with their followers close behind.

A good example is John Chrysostom. My college course in Church history taught that this fiery fourth-century preacher was a gifted rhetorician—known, in fact, as "golden mouthed." Cairns describes Chrysostom as a person who "did not always possess tact, but he did have a courteous, affectionate, kindly nature." Then, after describing his theologically sound exegetical methods, Cairns tells us, "He taught that there must be no divorce of morals and religion; the cross and ethics must go hand in hand."[41]

These quotations are taken from *Christianity Through the Centuries*, a well-known textbook which has been standard issue in evangelical colleges for many years. Look, now, at a different side of Chrysostom, the side that most evangelicals either do not know or choose not to discuss. Edward Flannery provides several documented quotations of Chrysostom's attitudes toward the Jewish people in his highly respected work on Christian anti-Semitism, *The Anguish of the Jews*. Mixing his own transitions with Chrysostom's words, Flannery writes:

> How can Christians dare "have the slightest converse" with the Jews, "most miserable of all men…men who are rapacious, greedy, perfidious bandits…ravenous murderers, destroyers, men possessed by the devil…." The Synagogue? It is the "domicile of the devil, as is also the soul of the Jews." Their religion is "a disease."

Because of all this and more, Chrysostom, the expert on ethics and morals, tells Christians:

> He who can never love Christ enough will never have done fighting against them [the Jews] who hate Him. Flee, then, their assemblies, flee their houses, and far from venerating the synagogue because of the books it contains hold it in hatred and aversion for the same reason. I hate the synagogue precisely because it has the law and the Prophets....I hate the Jews because they outrage the law.[42]

At the core of this hatred, according to Flannery, are the accusations that the Jews are Christ killers whose law should have no part in the life of the Christian. Indeed, there are many other documented examples of the hatred of the early Church toward the Jewish people, and toward the writings of Moshe as a way of life. It is true that the Torah was used to illustrate many truths about the Messiah. But after centuries of anti-Jewish, anti-Torah, and even anti-Semitic teaching from the most influential leaders of the Church, no one would dare attempt to follow one of its precepts or teach others to do the same.

Multiply the years, the decades, and the centuries. Changing a time-honored tradition can be extremely difficult, especially when those we love and respect see little need for such a change. This is especially true when discussing the interpretation of the passages in the Brit Chadasha that deal with the Torah. Unfortunately, we stand on centuries of anti-Torah tradition in the Church. One way to begin breaking that tradition is to examine how it became a tradition in the first place; thus the brief historical sketch above. You yourself can also begin to break destructive traditions and to establish new, honest and accurate interpretive traditions by dealing fairly and justly with God's Word.

Building Better Traditions—the Tradition of "Law"

There is another way to break a tradition of lies: we must begin to tell the truth. For our purposes, we will need to reexamine a few of the many passages in the Brit Chadasha which have been used to speak against the Torah. Rav Sha'ul of Tarsus is often looked upon as the culprit—the one who forsook Torah and began a new way of thinking about it. Let us now survey a few examples of his letters.

In addition to the historical precedent outlined above, anti-Torah interpretation of the Brit Chadasha can also be attributed to the misunderstanding of the Greek word *nomos*. This word is quite often translated "law." However, "In the Septuagint *nomos* occurs about 430 times...the commonest equivalent is *torah*....It is important to note that *torah* does *not* mean 'law' in the modern sense of the term."[43]

From this we learn that even though the writers of the Brit Chadasha translated the Hebrew word *torah* with a Greek word, *nomos*, which could mean "law," the intended meaning behind that word was most often *torah*, or in English, "teaching." But when prevailing theological tradition holds that the Torah is no longer valid as a way of life for the believer in Yeshua, the natural way of translating *nomos* is with its secular equivalent of "law." Thus, we have the linguistic concept of "law" born in the Brit Chadasha. However, "law" is not merely an erroneous way of translating the Hebrew concept of *torah*; it constitutes an erroneous theological idea all in itself. This idea could be termed "justification by works"—a system which requires us to do, or not do, certain things in order to be justified in His sight.

Performance-Based Acceptance

Sinful man has always had a tendency to take God's teachings and make laws out of them. He does this because, in his depraved state, he thinks that the only way to receive or retain God's acceptance is to earn it by meeting some standard of behavior. (Incidentally, this legalistic tendency is not restricted to God's Torah; it can be applied to any teaching on the subject of righteousness.) Thus, man has taken God's written expression of His heart and mind and perverted it into a list of rules which, obeyed to the letter, promise to win him the approval of the Almighty. Furthermore, he has added to this system of acceptable behavior a second list of rules which he himself has devised.

This system of performance-based acceptance is embraced by man as his "religion." Man-made religion seeks to reduce God's Word to a set of laws and regulations which require us to perform. It also attempts to rate our worth before God according to how *well* we perform. However, the Torah of God gives us the freedom to be the new creations He has made us to be—those who walk by faith, in an intimate relationship with our Father and with our Bridegroom.

Unfortunately, many in the Body have unwittingly fallen into the "law" tradition as well. Although aware of the grace of God, these believers nonetheless feel that God might not continue to love them, or save them, unless they obey some list of rules. This also is called law. Thus, the same fate has befallen these believers as the unbelievers: they have confused God's Torah with man-made, religious-looking laws.

Again, one reason for this confusion is the mistranslation of the word *nomos* in the Brit Chadasha. Instead of accurately rendering it as *torah*, the translators persisted in their centuries-old belief that the Torah of Moshe has little place—if any—in the life of Yeshua's followers. Hence, they have chosen the word "law" where *torah* would have been the accurate translation.

Problem Phrases—the Book of Galatians

Another factor contributing to the misinterpretation of Rav Sha'ul is the language he uses, especially in Romans and Galatians, in discussing the believer's relationship to the Torah. We have two specific phrases in mind: *upo nomen* ("under the law") and *erga nomou* ("works of the law"). When Sha'ul uses these terms, it is generally in a rather negative light.

Look, for example, at Romans 6:14, which reads, "For you are not *under law* but under grace [italics ours]." Here Sha'ul is stressing that the believer in Yeshua is dependent on Messiah for his salvation, which he can only receive through the grace of God. An example of the second phrase, "works of the law," is found in Galatians 2:16, "knowing that a man is not justified by works of law, but by the faith of Yeshua the Messiah." Whatever "works of law" means, it is clearly being used in a negative sense, denoting something opposed to having faith in Yeshua for salvation. Indeed, Sha'ul rebuked the Galatians for trusting in works of law.

In these passages, Sha'ul was teaching against *legalism*—the attempt to earn, merit, or keep one's salvation through obedience to law. But there were no sufficient words to express "legalism." Instead he had to use certain phrases which, interpreted incorrectly, could easily lead one to believe that he was against the Torah.

C. E. B. Cranfield has shed much light on the meaning of these two Greek phrases, helping us to perceive what Sha'ul actually meant as well as to understand more fully his true stand on the Torah. Because Cranfield's remarks are so pertinent we will quote him at length:

> It will be well to bear in mind the fact (which, as far as we know, had not received attention before it was noted)...that the Greek language of Paul's day possessed no word-group corresponding to our "legalism," "legalist," and "legalistic." This means that he lacked a convenient terminology for expressing a vital distinction, and so was surely seriously hampered in the work of clarifying the Christian position with regard to the law. In view of this we should

always, we think, be ready to reckon with the possibility that Pauline statements, which at first sight seem to disparage the law, are really directed not against the law itself but against that misunderstanding and misuse of it for which we now have a convenient terminology. In this very difficult terrain Paul was pioneering. If we make due allowance for these circumstances, we shall not be so easily baffled or misled by a certain impreciseness of statement which we shall sometimes encounter.[44]

We encounter the same dilemma in the Hebrew language. There are no Hebrew words which can easily convey the concepts of "legalism" or "legalist." Thus Sha'ul, whether using his Hebrew-oriented mind or his Greek language, was hindered in his attempts to explain that legalism was not what God intended. From our understanding of the true nature of the Torah and Rav Sha'ul's theology, it is our opinion that he did an excellent job of overcoming this language barrier!

The next detrimental theological tradition we must bring to light is the long-standing misinterpretation of *nomos/torah* in the Book of Galatians. This is the book that says, "But if you are led by the Spirit, you are not under the law" (5:18). Moreover, such people have "fallen from grace" (5:4). In addition, "I, Paul, say to you that if you receive circumcision, Christ will be of no benefit to you" (5:2).

These rather harsh-sounding statements, among a host of others in this lett, have been used for centuries against any believer who desired to follow the Torah—especially in regard to circumcision, Shabbat observance, or any other non-moral issue. What are we to make of them?

The explanation is rather simple; all we need to know are two basic facts. The first is the hermeneutical principle established by Acts 21:20ff. If it appears that Sha'ul was teaching against the Torah in any way, that impression must give way to the truth of how he lived his life. If Acts 21 tells us that Sha'ul lived his life according to the Torah and encouraged others to do the same, then we will miss the boat if we interpret Galatians as coming from an anti-Torah viewpoint.

The second fact to bear in mind is the hermeneutical principle of *context*, especially the context of the whole book. To be specific, the context of the letter to the Galatians is that of justification by faith. Sha'ul was warning them not to make a "law" out of the Torah. By turning God's teaching and covenant into a list of legalistic laws, the Galatians were abandoning the principle of justification by faith and resorting to justification by works. They were using the Torah as a means of earning, meriting, or keeping the eternal salvation which they had received by grace through faith in the finished work of Yeshua.

Sha'ul provides several indications that this was the case with the Galatians. The first is in 2:16, "nevertheless knowing that a man is not justified by the works of the law, but through faith in Messiah Yeshua, even we have believed in Messiah Yeshua, that we may be justified by faith in Messiah, and not by the works of the law; since by the works of the law shall no flesh be justified." The issue on Sha'ul's mind was God's requirement for our justification.

Looking at the Greek of Galatians 2:16, we find that the definite article before the phrase "works of law" has been left out. It is not, as many English versions translate it, "works of the law." If the translator adds the definite article, it helps the reader to *assume* that "the law" is a reference to the Torah. In fact, however, it is not. "Works of law" is a phrase indicating a man-made system of works, of which performance-based acceptance is the core belief. *Ergon nomou* should be translated as "works of law."

Thus, Galatians 2:16 should read: "knowing that a man is not justified by works of law but through faith in Messiah

Yeshua, even we have believed in Messiah Yeshua, that we may be justified by faith in Messiah, and not by works of law; since by works of law shall no flesh be justified."

Galatians 5:4 reads, "You have been severed from Messiah, you who are seeking to be justified by law; you have fallen from grace." Many use this verse to demonstrate that those who follow the Torah have fallen from the grace of God because they are obeying the "law" instead of Messiah—who, it is argued, set them free from the law. In defense of this position, they cite the context (verses 2–3): "Behold I, Paul, say to you that if you receive circumcision, Messiah will be of no benefit to you. And I testify again to every man who receives circumcision, that he is under obligation to keep the whole law." They say, "If you do what the Torah says and circumcise your sons, you are no longer following Yeshua."

Our response? Sha'ul himself provides the key for the correct understanding of this passage in verse 4, in which he tells us that anyone who observes Torah while "seeking to be justified by law" will encounter serious difficulties.

Some of the Galatians thought that obeying the Torah (or any set of standards) would cause them to receive their spiritual heritage—justification before God. However, the moment a person believes that obedience can secure righteousness, he has moved from the realm of grace into that of works. The blessings of God, he thinks, are attainable as a result of what he does.

Sha'ul, on the other hand, says that such a person has fallen from the principle of grace to the principle of "law." In effect, when one believes such an erroneous teaching, the atonement accomplished by Yeshua has no value for him, since he is relying on what he does instead of what Yeshua did for him.

The teachings of the Torah were never intended to be used for such a purpose. Eternal salvation is based on receiving the promises of God, which are given by grace to those who do not deserve them. The only acceptable response to this grace is to receive it by faith, rather than attempt to earn it by *doing* something. If we obey the Torah in order to enjoy the blessings of the grace of God received by faith, we are not "fallen from grace"; rather, we are embracing the grace of God for our lives. Put another way, if man tries to earn the blessings of God instead of appropriating Messiah's life, he has abandoned the principle of grace and fallen to the principle of "law." To live the Torah is to live our new creation life in Messiah: it is actually His life in us, a life of grace and truth. Thus the Torah is God's revelation to those born of Him, concerning how they are to act in line with the truth of the Good News. (Galatians 2:14)

Real biblical faith is the kind of trust in God that *always* results in a changed life. The Torah (as well as the Brit Chadasha) describes what that changed life looks like. It does not *cause* that changed life. That is the miraculous work of God, born of His grace.

We must leave Galatians now. Our point was to establish the fact that the statements in the letter which seem to teach against the Torah are not against it at all if one uses the Torah properly. There were some Galatians who were turning Torah into "law" by using it as a means of justification rather than as a way of life resulting from their justification. Let us turn now to the Book of Romans.

The theme of Sha'ul's letter to the Romans is similar to that of his epistle to the Galatians, only more comprehensive. The main topic is justification, or righteousness (the same root is used for both in Hebrew and Greek). In Romans, the rabbi is seeking to expound on the theme of God's righteousness in all its various aspects. As in Galatians, he also must deal with the concept of the Torah, for there were some in Rome as well who sought to be justified or made righteous by following the system of law that they thought was the Torah.

Since the themes are similar, the traditions of interpretation of the "law passages" are also similar. The Church has consisted mostly of non-Jews throughout the centuries, most of whom have neither comprehended nor appreciated the Torah of Moshe. Therefore they have taken little care to interpret the "law passages" properly. There are two key passages in Romans which have been especially misunderstood by many exegetes, resulting in a gross anti-Torah sentiment among the people of God.

The first is in Romans 10:4: "For Messiah is the end of the law for righteousness to everyone who believes." Many understand this verse to mean that Yeshua put an end to the Torah; that anyone who believes in Him no longer has any responsibility to follow the Torah, because Yeshua followed it for him.

A closer look at the Greek, however, reveals a different meaning. The Greek word translated "end" is the word *telos.* This word actually stresses the "goal" or purpose for something. When used in this verse, we can say that Messiah is the "goal (*telos*) of the law."[45] Or, as Stern translates it, "Messiah is the goal at which the Torah aims." In other words, in the context, Sha'ul is speaking of people seeking the righteousness of God. They should seek it as revealed in the Torah and most fully realized in the Messiah. Stern writes,

> The goal at which the Torah aims is acknowledging and trusting in the Messiah, who offers on the ground of this trusting the very righteousness they are seeking. They would see that the righteousness which the Torah offers is offered through Him and only through Him.[46]

Thus, instead of teaching that through faith in Messiah the Torah is now done away with, this verse teaches that the Torah's goal is to point someone to the righteousness found through faith in Messiah. A sinner can only be made righteous through faith in the Messiah. However, as a new creation in Messiah after receiving Yeshua, he is now able to live the Torah lifestyle through the power of the indwelling Spirit of God. In so doing, he is living out who he now is— the righteousness of God in Messiah. The Torah is the revealed righteousness of God. The Torah lifestyle is the living out of that righteousness. What is it that is written on the new-creation heart and mind? The very Torah of God! (Jeremiah 31:33)

Finally, we will look at one of the passages most commonly used to demonstrate that the believer has no responsibility to follow the Torah: the seventh chapter of the Book of Romans. To be sure, this is a difficult passage to understand completely. However, it can be interpreted accurately enough to confirm that it has nothing to do with eliminating a believer's responsibility to live the Torah, to live the righteousness of God that he has become as a new creation in Messiah.

The key questions that we must ask about this passage are these: What has died? What has changed? Was it the Torah that died, or was it something else? We ask these questions because the first half of the chapter speaks about a death, a separation, a change that occurred when Messiah came into our lives.

We know from reading Matthew 5:17ff that the Torah could not have died. It is God's eternal Word! Therefore, something else must have died. What has changed is our *relationship* to the Torah, because of our changed relationship to sin. Before we knew Messiah's righteousness by faith, we attempted to use the Torah as a means of earning righteousness, something it was never intended to be. Only one outcome could have resulted from such an illegitimate usage, and that is condemnation—because such works-righteousness could never remove our sin.

When God brought us to faith in Messiah, however, everything changed. By faith, we transferred our trust from works we attempted to do ourselves to the finished work of Yeshua. Our new reality is that Messiah has atoned for our sin and made us new creations. In other words, we submitted to God's righteousness found in Yeshua instead of relying on man's righteousness through our own efforts.

Thus, our relationship to the Torah has changed. Before, because we were using it wrongly by attempting to earn our justification through following it, all the Torah could do was condemn us. Now, because we believe in Messiah and are trusting in God to justify us, the Torah has become something completely different. Just as its Author designed it to be, it is "holy, righteous, and good." (Romans 7:12)

Our relationship to the Torah can change, according to Sha'ul, because the problem was not the Torah—it was sin. "Therefore, did that which is good [Torah] become a cause of death for me? May it never be! Rather it was *sin*, in order that it might be shown to be *sin* by effecting my death through that which is good, that through the commandment *sin* might become utterly *sinful*." (Romans 7:13)

For years, many have been hearing a different interpretation of this crucial passage. Now we want a new voice to be heard. Listen to it one more time as a summary. This passage teaches that our real enemy was sin, not the Torah. Because we are new creations in Messiah, our entire relationship to sin has changed. Therefore, our entire relationship to the Torah has changed. Before Messiah, sin caused the Torah to be a book which, because we followed it in an attempt to earn righteousness, largely served to condemn us. But Messiah has shown us that we cannot earn righteousness. Rather, it is a gift from God to all who trust in the sacrificial atonement and subsequent resurrection of Messiah. Hence, after we trusted in Messiah, the Torah became for us what it was really meant to be all along: a holy, righteous, and good book.

Since they did not know the righteousness that comes from God

and sought to

establish their own righteousness

they did not submit to God's righteousness.

For an unredeemed (unregenerate) person to take the Torah and try to *do* it—to try to attain to the righteousness that only comes from God—

changes the Torah

from

Grace

Righteousness that comes from God (Romans 10:3)

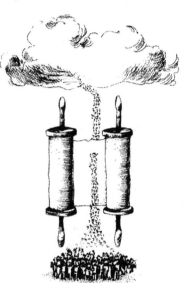

By this Torah you shall live.

to

Law

Man's attempt to establish his own righteousness (Romans 10:3)

By this law you shall be both judged and condemned.

"For they, being ignorant of God's righteousness, and seeking to establish their own righteousness, have not submitted to the righteousness of God." (Romans 10:3)

Summing it All Up

Let us conclude this chapter by returning to an image we introduced earlier, a powerful one which crystallizes everything we have been saying about the true Torah. We are speaking of the mirror analogy found in the first chapter of the Book of James.

The Mirror

The true Torah is our walk of faith. Faith is taking God at His Word regarding who He is and who we, His children, are—His bride and His people. The true Torah is for us a mirror, reflecting who we now are as ones who have been redeemed and made anew by the finished work of the Messiah.

Rav Sha'ul understood this completely, and carefully exposed the age-old legalistic tendency of men throughout his letters. Ya'acov adds to our understanding of the true Torah in his letter when he says, "Do not merely listen to the Word and so deceive yourselves. Do what it says." (James 1:22) Why? Because it is telling us who we are! How do we know that this is how Ya'acov understood the Torah? By his next statement in verse 23, "For if anyone is a hearer of the word and not a doer, he is like a man who looks at his natural face in a mirror; for once he has looked at himself and gone away, he has immediately forgotten what kind of person he was."

Notice what this is saying! When we read the Word and then do not do just what it says, we have looked at our own face in the mirror and then gone away and "forgotten" what we look like. The Word of God is the mirror in which we see who we now are—what we look like. Because the work of Messiah is a finished work, all that is left for us to do is to rejoice in the finished work of Messiah—our new creation self—and then "behave consistently" (our walk of faith) with who we now are. The true Torah tells us, like a mirror, what we "look like." That is, it tells us what behavior would be consistent with who we now are—the righteousness of God in Messiah! (Romans 5:19)

Torah is God's teaching to men about righteousness—what it is and how it behaves. The true believer (anyone who is redeemed by the blood of the Lamb) does not *do* in order to *become*. He does because he is what God has made him—the righteousness of God in Messiah. Thus Ya'acov writes, "I will show you my faith by my works." (James 2:18) The true Torah is the walk of faith—faith and rest in the finished work of Messiah. "This is what the Sovereign Lord, the Holy One of Israel, says, 'In repentance and rest is your salvation, in quietness and trust is your strength, but you would have none of it.'" (Isaiah 30:15) Instead, "Since they did not know the righteousness that comes from God, and sought to establish their own, they did not submit to God's righteousness." (Romans 10:3)

These words of Rav Sha'ul summarize perfectly why and how man has perverted the true Torah of God into a system of works by which he believes he can establish his own righteousness. Read the rabbi's words once again, and think about them carefully:

"Since they did not know the righteousness that comes from God, and sought to establish their own, they did not submit to God's righteousness."

Ya'acov, fully comprehending this, declares, "I will show you my faith by my works." (James 2:18) "The man who looks intently into the perfect Torah"—the what?—"the perfect Torah that gives freedom"—that gives what? Freedom! Freedom for what? Freedom to be who we now are!—"and continues to do this, not forgetting who he is but doing who he is—he will be blessed in what he does." (James 1:25, our paraphrase)

There is a righteousness that is by the Torah (Romans 10:5). It is a righteousness that is ours in God (Romans 10:3), and it is by faith (Romans 10:6). This is the Good News of Romans 10:16. But not all the Israelites accepted the Good News. Instead they, and mankind throughout the ages, have developed the concept of "law." As we have seen, performance-based acceptance is a detrimental theological idea all in itself.

Building Better Traditions

"Thus says the Lord, 'Stand at the crossroads and look; ask for the ancient paths, ask where the good way is, and walk in it; and you shall find rest for your souls.' But you said, 'We will not walk in it!'" (Jeremiah 6:16) The true Torah is "a tree of life to those who embrace her; those who lay hold of her will be blessed. Long life is in her right hand; in her left hand are riches and honor. Her ways are pleasant ways, and all her paths are peace." (Proverbs 3:16–18)

When the words of life (true Torah) are changed into "law," they cease to be the words of life. Let us be very clear! Striving and toiling are the identifying marks of Satan's kingdom. Dwelling in delight and rest are the identifying marks of God's kingdom.

Will the true Torah please stand up?

Epilogue

Epilogue

We would like to conclude this book by speaking some personal words to two different groups of people: Jewish believers in Yeshua and non-Jewish believers in Yeshua.

To the "People of the Book"

That's right, that's what they call us Jewish people. We have been known throughout the centuries as the *People of the Book*. What book? What book other than the Torah has been such a source of strength and comfort for our people? What other book has served as the body of teachings which have given us identity as a nation and as a people? What book has been the object of study for our sages, shoemakers, seamstresses, and schoolteachers, but the Torah?

If the Torah has always been the book which held our people together in the past, how much more so should it be for us, the remnant of those who are chosen by grace to believe in the Messiah? This was His book, too! The Torah was the book of all of His early followers. It was the book that formed the basis of all of their teaching as it is reflected in the Brit Chadasha—the best commentary on the Torah ever written, and the only one which is the inspired Word of God.

We have seen how theological error and misinterpretation of the Brit Chadasha have led to an outright neglect of the Torah at best, and a stiff-necked rejection of it at worst. Let us now attempt to do what no other generation has ever done. Let us be the first generation of Jewish believers since the early days of our history to begin turning back the tear-drenched pages of our history and again to follow the covenant which the Holy One made with Moshe Rabbenu. Let us begin to live faithfully the sacred marriage agreement which the Heavenly Bridegroom signed, sealed, and delivered to our ancestors in the wilderness of Sinai. After all, we are His bride! We are redeemed! We are new creations! We have the Spirit of God empowering us to live out the words of life!

One of our goals in writing this book is to stir in Jewish believers, particularly, a sense of excitement and responsibility in following the Torah, as it is written on the pages of the sacred scrolls. This is not a halachic treatise. It is a book on the basics of the nature of Torah, striving to remind us of who we are as Jewish people who believe in Yeshua. May it spur you on to study more and continue to work out a Messianic Jewish halacha which takes into account both the Brit Chadasha and the Torah. We hope to see many more volumes written in this regard. More than that, however, we hope to see many Messianic Jewish believers changed, walking as new creations whose lives reflect the instructions both in the pages of Torah and in the Brit Chadasha—the way God intended us to walk all along—the way of Yeshua the Messiah, the living Torah. Why? Because it is who we are!

To Those Grafted In

For you, one of our goals is to demonstrate the theological validity of living a Torah-oriented lifestyle for the believer in Yeshua. If you think this has little to do with you, at least encourage your Jewish brothers and sisters to follow the divine covenant they were given by grace.

But we think that the Torah has much to do with you. We want you to realize that the Torah (as well as the rest of the Tenach) forms the basis of every teaching found in the Brit Chadasha. Moreover, the Brit Chadasha, because of progressive revelation, fully explains all of the seed concepts found in the Torah. In short, the two were not meant to be contradictory, but rather to fit hand in glove.

We hope we have demonstrated that the Torah was never intended to be a salvation document. Instead, it was designed by the Holy One to be the basis of the redeemed lifestyle for God's holy community. Where Torah has been used as a means of salvation, we have clearly shown that the only function it can serve, in such cases, is to condemn man by revealing his sin and his need for an atoning Messiah.

What part do you play? You make the decision. Here are the facts concerning yourself: You are a new creation in Yeshua. That means, according to Jeremiah 31:33, that the Torah is written upon your new-creation heart. Moreover, the Messiah who indwells you is the Torah and His life lived out through man is the Torah lifestyle. Messiah's life in you is the living Torah living out His life through you on earth.

If you are a new creation in Messiah, "these words [the Torah as given on Mount Sinai] are not just idle words for you, they are your life." (Deuteronomy 32:47) In the same way that Yeshua is your life, the words of Torah are your life.

How can this be? It is the only thing that can be true, because the written Torah and the living Torah are one and the same! "And the Torah (Word) became flesh and dwelt among us...." (John 1:14, our paraphrase)

When we ask, "Will the true Torah please stand up," what we want to leave with you is the thought that as you live the Torah, Messiah Himself will stand up in you and through you for all to see. When those around you have seen Him, they have seen the Father (John 14:9). Remember, the Torah, both written and living, *is* a revelation of the righteousness of God to men. Embracing the Torah and living it allow Messiah Himself, the true Torah, to stand up!

Furthermore, you are not Jewish people if your physical ancestry cannot be traced back to Abraham through Isaac and Jacob. But, on the other hand, Rav Sha'ul tells us in Romans 11 and Ephesians 2 that non-Jewish believers in Yeshua are "grafted in" to "the commonwealth of Israel." Certainly, among other things, the teachings which give Israel national identity also give you identity.

It is important to notice in Acts 15 the wisdom of the earliest followers of Yeshua when they were gathered in conference in Jerusalem. They knew it was not necessary or wise to require a complete and instant Torah lifestyle for those who would be new at it, such as the new believers from among the Gentiles. Instead, they made it clear that they understood these new believers would be gathered together in the synagogue, every Shabbat and week by week. There they would hear instruction concerning their new-creation life through the reading and teaching of the Torah. They knew the teaching of their Master. "The sheep hear My voice and follow Me....I have other sheep that are not of this sheep pen [the Jewish sheep pen]. I must bring them also [those chosen from among the Gentiles]. They too will listen to My voice, and there shall be one flock and one shepherd." (John 10:17, 27—explanation ours)

One life—His life! One lifestyle—the righteousness of God! In reality, if we understand the Torah properly, how can anyone resist it? Who would want to miss out on the joys of Passover and Succot? Who would want to be denied the blessings of demonstrating the deep biblical symbolism of affixing a mezuzah or wearing fringes? Who would ever want to deny any true believer the privileges and blessings of following the Torah?

In addition, do we not all agree with Rav Sha'ul that the Torah is "inspired by God and profitable for teaching, for reproof, for correction, for training in righteousness; that the man of God may be adequate, equipped for every good work"? Most think that II Timothy 3:16–17 is speaking about the Brit Chadasha. In reality, however, the only Scripture Sha'ul had available to him was the Tenach, which included the Torah. The Brit Chadasha had not yet been compiled!

Are you beginning to see that you have more of a practical relationship to the Torah than you ever realized? Dig deeper! Follow it closer, and see how much more it can enrich your life.

To All

When the Torah scroll is taken out of the ark during the synagogue service, it is paraded around as the congregation praises God for giving them such revelation. Then it is read and studied. But just before it is stored away until the next Torah service, someone raises the Torah high above all, for everyone to see, as if raising his hands to the Holy One in worship. As he does this, the entire congregation sings:

"This is the Torah that Moshe placed before the children of Israel; upon the command of the Lord, through Moshe's hand. *It is a tree of life for those who grasp it, and its supporters are praiseworthy. Its ways are ways of pleasantness, and all its paths are peace....*"

In what way is the Torah a "tree of life"? It has been the intention of this book to lay the foundation for us to discover that secret. With God's help, other volumes will follow which will bring to light that spiritual gold mine. We also hope to produce group study packages as a help to those of you who desire to discover in this "tree of life" the words of life for the redeemed.

Years ago, Hilkiah the high priest rediscovered the Torah as he was rummaging through God's Holy House. He found it there, deep within the confines of the Temple. In the same way, deep within the confines of the temple of our new-creation hearts, we can rediscover that same treasure. "But we have this treasure in jars of clay to show that this all-surpassing power is from God and not from us." (II Corinthians 4:7) It is there, inscribed on our hearts forever by the Spirit of God. Just look, and you will also rediscover it for yourself. When you do, may you see it as it truly is, the written revelation of the life of grace in the Messiah, the living embodiment of its pages.

"...I offer you this day life and death, now choose life..."

Deuteronomy 30:19

LIFE
through
CHOICE

The Torah reveals the truth, showing us the differences between holy and unholy, pure and impure, and between life and death.

It is, therefore, the grace of God.

Embracing the goodness of God
for your life.

Appendixes

Appendix A
How to Study and Teach Torah

One of our desires in writing this book was to inspire you to begin to study Torah, the first five books of the Bible, for yourself. Once you embark on your study, you will soon realize what everyone who has attempted to learn the truths in the Torah has already discovered: it isn't easy! The purpose of this appendix is to help you along the way with some important pointers which should make your study easier and more rewarding.

There are three kinds of material in this section. The first is a set of principles which will help you to more accurately interpret the Torah. Scholars call this field of study *hermeneutics*—the study of how to interpret. The second part of this section deals with practical methods which will help you to organize your studies for yourself. In addition, it will also help equip you to better communicate your findings to others. In the final section, we will offer some suggestions about which study aids may help you most.

How to Interpret the Torah

When we seek to understand the Torah, we must bear in mind several goals. We will list these randomly because, in reality, each is just as important as the other.

To Be Built Up

The first goal is to train up the man and woman of God. One of the greatest Torah scholars, Sha'ul of Tarsus, wrote these instructions to a student of his when he was training him for ministry. Sha'ul said in II Timothy 3:16:

All Scripture is inspired by God and profitable for teaching, for reproof, for correction, and for training in righteousness; that the man of God may be adequate, equipped for every good work.

When Sha'ul said that "all" Scripture had usefulness in the lives of believers, he would also have included the Torah. Hence, along with the rest of the Scriptures, the Torah also is profitable for teaching, for reproving, for correcting, and for training people in righteousness. In the end, the ultimate goal of all of these things is that the people of God would be built up and thoroughly equipped to serve God.

To See the Messiah

The second goal of our Torah study is that we might be able to see the Messiah clearly in its pages. Remember Luke 24. This chapter establishes for us one of the key hermeneutic principles of approaching Torah. Here Yeshua tells us specifically to look in the Torah in order to see Him.

And beginning with Moshe and with all the prophets, He explained to them the things concerning Himself in all the Scriptures. (Luke 24:27)

When I first started looking for Yeshua in every parasha, I worried I would come across one so legally oriented that I wouldn't be able to find Yeshua anywhere. However, much to my surprise, after beginning the work I found it difficult to stop! I have discovered that the person and work of Messiah are evident in even the most technical sections of the Torah. And the more we see Him, the more we can worship Him.

To Teach Others

The last goal we will mention is, of course, to teach the Torah to others. That means that not only should you learn a method of study for yourself, but you should also learn a method which will enable you to put all of your Torah discoveries in a nice, neat package in order to teach somebody else.

Go by the Rules!

There are commonly accepted rules for proper interpretation of the Scriptures. These rules also apply to the Torah. For a more detailed explanation on each of these, you can easily purchase several types of books on how to understand the Bible. We highly recommend that you do so.

Before listing some of the most important hermeneutical rules, we need to clarify an important point. There are sometimes vast differences of opinion between evangelical and rabbinic rules of interpretation. To be sure, there are also important similarities. For example, take your *siddur* and look up "Rabbi Ishmael's 13 Rules of Interpretation" (beginning on page 49 of the *Ashkenaz Complete ArtScroll Siddur Kol Yakov*), or even look up Rabbi Eleazar's "32 Principles of Interpretation." In both of these lists, there are a multitude of principles of biblical interpretation which are accepted by both groups—and so it ought to be.

But sometimes there are marked differences as well. For example, the rabbis hold to the use of gematria as a valid and important interpretive rule. Gematria is the practice of finding meanings in the words and letters of the Torah by calculating their numerical value. Most of the time it is not as simple as this definition makes it sound. In fact, the practice of gematria can be extremely complex and sometimes arbitrary. For this reason we do not recommend that a student of Torah regard the findings of gematria as authoritative interpretation.

In addition to gematria, the rabbis also seek to find the allegorical or "hidden meanings" of the text of the Torah. (This is sometimes called "making a *midrash.*") Once again, because these "hidden meanings" can also be rather speculative, we do not recommend that the serious Torah student practice the midrashic method of interpretation.

To be sure, the findings of both gematria and midrash can be, at times, extremely fascinating. For the most part, those who practice such methods usually intend them to contribute to the fuller meaning of a text. However, for the reasons suggested above, we suggest that the study of the Torah does not require the student to use them. The Torah is full of deep and beautiful meanings even without the use of such methods.

All of these cautions aside, here is a list of some of the most important hermeneutical rules which the Torah student should practice.

1. Rely on the Spirit of God to be your teacher.

One of our favorite prayers for beginning a study of the Torah is a quote from Psalm 119:18, which says, "Open my eyes, that I might behold wonderful things from Your Torah." We need to remember that since it is God's words we are studying, only God, through His Spirit, can cause us to understand them.

2. Determine which kind of literature it is that you are studying.

The five books of the Torah contain just about every type of literature imaginable, including *historical narrative, legal material, poems,* and *songs.* As Torah students, we need to be aware of which kind of literature we are studying. For example, the way we would interpret the story of Abraham in Genesis 12 would differ slightly from how we would interpret the rules on cleanliness in Leviticus 11 and 12. Thus, the type of literature studied will determine how we study it.

3. We must become experts in the text.

This means several things. First and foremost, it means we need to become thoroughly familiar with the *contents* of the text. We know it may sound like a boring exercise, but before we do any kind of interpreting of the text we must read it repeatedly to be sure we have not missed any important details of the passage. One of the mistakes people make in interpreting Scripture, especially Torah, is doing it too quickly. In our haste, we simply miss too many important details of the passage. In short, we need to practice the fine art of careful observation.

Once upon a time, in a biology class taught by one Professor Aziz, sat a student who was interested in becoming a great scientist. To begin his training, the professor slapped a fish down before him and said, "Here is a fish. Observe it!" After about half an hour the student, having jotted down a few observations about the fish, gave his one-page list to the professor. Upon reading it, the wise teacher muttered, "Nice job, but you've barely begun. Go back to the fish and observe some more."

Several hours passed as the young student recorded more and more details. He took his findings a second time to the professor, who responded by saying, "That's great, but you've only scratched the surface! Now, how about taking a *real* look at that fish?"

The hours turned into a day, the day into many days, until the student returned to the professor one more time. This time he brought almost a book full of details concerning every single facet of the fish. He described the way each of the fish's fins curled, the various shades of color in its scales, the texture of its tail, and many more features he had painstakingly noted. The professor, looking more pleased by now, told the student that because he was finally learning the art of careful observation, his desired career of being a scientist had just begun!

The point of the story is obvious. We, too, are science students. Our "field" of study is the Scriptures. If a professor can require his students to be diligent in their observations of fish, surely the wise Teacher Himself would desire that we make even more careful observations concerning what He wrote in the Torah—as well as in the rest of the Word of God—about Himself.

There are six key words which will help us to improve our observation skills. We need to ask: *who, what, where, when, why,* and *how* about everything we encounter in a given text of the Torah. These questions words will help us dig out the details of the passage.

Those who teach *inductive* Bible study methods (which are essentially what we are espousing here) call this the *observation* stage of our study. Before we begin to decide what a passage *means*, we must first know what it *says*.

4. Context

Observing the context is one of the most fundamental rules of interpreting any piece of literature. This is especially true of interpreting the Torah. Even the so-called "teaching sections" have some kind of important context. Watch out for it, and try to determine what the context is for any and every given passage you are studying.

There are several kinds of contexts. There is, first of all, the context of the *whole book*. If we are studying Genesis, for example, and we come upon an instructional section, we need to remember that Genesis is basically historical narrative. We must understand these instructions, then, in light of the history being unfolded in the context of the whole book. Furthermore, when studying an instructional section like Leviticus which has little historical narration, it is necessary to consider the possibility that God is giving these instructions because of some historical event in Israel's life which prompted either correction or further instruction.

Second, there is the *paragraph* or *section* in which our text is located. For example, part of the reason Leviticus 16 was written was to explain about the blood and the sacrifices for Yom Kippur. But another purpose was to remind Israel of who could approach God, and in what manner He could be approached. This instruction was necessary in order to ensure that the incident involving Nadav and Avihu (Nadab and Abihu) would not happen again.

Finally, there is the *immediate context*. This is the material which immediately precedes or follows the section we are studying. The whole meaning of a text can be lost because of the failure of a student to observe its immediate context. In short, it behooves us to pay close attention to all contexts of any passage we choose to study.

One more point. Remember that both chapter and verse divisions and weekly parasha divisions are man-made! This means that one of these divisions may throw you off in attempting to determine a context. Be on the lookout for this. Do not let man-made divisions in the Torah text rule your understanding of a passage.

5. Understand the text at face value. Avoid the temptation to allegorize.

By instructing you to take the text at face value, we mean that if we are dealing with poetry, then we have a license to find symbolic meanings. Otherwise, the text is meant to be understood quite literally. For example, if the text says, "I am the Lord your God who brought you out of the land of Egypt and you are My people Israel and I am taking you to the land of the Canaanites," we are not to understand it as a charge to conquer the world or to move on to greater and higher adventures for God! On the contrary, the passage is talking about a literal God, telling a literal group of people called Israelites that He is taking them to a literal piece of real estate, which in that day was called the land of Canaan.

This also applies to what appear to be legal sections. If God said to put a fence around the top of your house, for example, He does not mean to build fences to protect the Torah! Literally, what is being referred to is a protective enclosure being placed around the top of a house to prevent people from falling off. (In that part of the world, most dwellings had flat roofs, which facilitated people congregating on them.) We have no permission at this point to go beyond the literal face value of the text.

Also associated with this principle is the necessity of determining the intended meaning of the passage. Since Moshe was the writer of the Torah, we must try to put ourselves in his shoes as he wrote it, even as we attempt to discern the Lord's intent in giving each teaching.

Perhaps we can clarify something important here. There is a big difference between saying "this passage means such and such" and saying "this passage *can serve as an illustration of* such and such." The former statement assigns a specifically intended meaning to the passage. The latter is merely saying that the passage *might* help us to understand another passage or concept.

We may only say that a given passage *means* something if we have thoroughly determined, through careful observation and application of the context, its original, God-intended meaning. However, we may use almost any passage to illustrate a spiritual principle without declaring it to be the original purpose for the passage.

For example, let us look at the passage describing the garments of the high priest and the different colors he wore. The text does not state the symbolic meaning of these colors, nor that the colors even *had* a symbolic meaning. To state that these colors mean *X*, *Y*, and *Z* is to practice *spiritualization*. It *is* legitimate, however, to say that each color can be seen as an illustration of something concerning our life in the Messiah (the blue reminds us of royalty, the white suggests purity, and so forth). Now, rather than definitively stating that the high priest's garments carried the symbolic meanings we have assigned them, we are merely observing that they can aptly illustrate certain spiritual truths. Do you see the difference?

Often we spiritualize or allegorize when attempting to apply a passage of Scripture to our lives. Practical application should be the *last* step in our study of the passage. When the time comes to personally apply the passage to our lives, we often make a dishonest mistake in handling it. We can best explain this mistake by giving an illustration. Let us look at Joshua, for instance. In typical applications, many people would say something like this: "We are all Joshuas. We are in the days of Joshua. We can all conquer the land for the Lord."

Unfortunately, such teaching is dishonest to the text. We are not all named Joshua. Moreover, who says we are in the days of Joshua? Do we ride chariots? Are there Canaanites living around us? Furthermore, did God give us all a mandate to take up swords, form an army, and conquer the land of Germany, South Africa, or the United States—or wherever else we may be living?

However, we *can* say, *"Just as* in the days of Joshua, *so also* in our days...."* The key phrases we want to use here are *"Just as" and "so also...."* We can draw many examples of what God did in Joshua's days to illustrate what He might be doing today.

We know this sounds like a complicated point, but it is important. We want to be fair and true to the text of Scripture because it is God's Word. We should not arbitrarily assign meanings to the Bible which are not warranted.

6. Know the historical, geographical, cultural, and religious backgrounds of the passage.

We cannot say too much on this point. The Torah was written in a historical, cultural, social, religious, and geographical context far removed from ours. We cannot even think of understanding it properly unless we are sufficiently familiar with these factors.

For example, it makes a difference to our understanding of the Torah if we know that each of the ten plagues was brought against one of the gods of Egypt. It changes our perception of the book of Deuteronomy if we are aware that its format virtually follows that of other late bronze age suzerain treaties and covenants. Moreover, are we aware that our knowledge of ancient Mesopotamian clay tablets can help us understand the structure of Genesis, as well as why Rachel stole the family idols from Laban?

A knowledge of the ancient Near East can open up the meaning of the Torah in ways that most people would never imagine. We would even suggest that a student who ignores this area of knowledge risks grossly misinterpreting the Torah, as he will never be able to fully appreciate the depth of the revelation found therein. This principle of Torah study is that important.

Closely connected with this rule is the principle of studying the Torah in Hebrew, its original language. There are sometimes words, thoughts, or concepts in the Hebrew of the Torah that are almost impossible to express in a translation. For example, it is helpful to know that the Hebrew word sometimes translated into English as "sacrifice" is the word *korban* (קרבן), which has the same root as the word meaning "to draw close." Hence, a sacrifice is that which helps us draw close to God. In addition, there are virtually no English equivalents for the Hebrew words *tahor* and *tamei* (often rendered pure and impure, or clean and unclean, respectively).

While it is difficult for most people to learn biblical Hebrew or to know the background of the Torah, there are many study aids which can assist the novice in these pursuits. Nothing can substitute for a working knowledge of both biblical Hebrew and ancient Near Eastern history.

Here, then, are the six basic hermeneutical rules which need to govern our study of the Bible. We can apply these rules to our study of any part of it.

1. Rely on the Spirit of God to be your teacher.
2. Determine which kind of literature you are studying.
3. Become an expert in the text.
4. Consider the context.
5. Understand the text at face value. Avoid the temptation to allegorize.
6. Know the historical, geographical, cultural, and religious backgrounds of the passage.

Specifically the Torah

The Torah contains some unique material which we will call *teaching sections*. Most of the Tenach does not contain this type of content. Therefore, in addition to the above rules, we also need to know the following specific suggestions for studying these unique types of passages in the Torah. We will repeat at least two of the above principles because of their special application to the study of the teaching sections of the Torah.

1. Context.

There is a definite context to most if not all of the long passages of teaching and instruction which so characterize the Torah. To be sure, it is sometimes rather difficult to determine the specific historical or literary context. But remember that the Torah was not given out of a vacuum. To understand it properly, we need to discern a context for each section.

Let us take the concept of blood, for example. The instructions about blood, whether human or animal, are a major feature of the book of Leviticus. When we look at the teaching passages, therefore, we need to ask why God is teaching about blood in this particular passage, as well as what these specific teachings add to the context of the whole book of Leviticus.

2. Historical background.

This is highly critical when we study the teaching sections of the Torah. God had definite reasons for giving each of His teachings, some of which arose out of certain situations taking place outside of its pages. We need to become aware of these background circumstances in order to understand these sections completely.

Here is an excellent example. The text says, "and you shall not shave the corners of your head." To understand this passage properly, we must first determine from the Hebrew what the text means. Second, we must ask ourselves a question: "Why would God have given that instruction?" Is He telling us how to get haircuts? What was happening historically at that time that would necessitate special instructions from the Holy One about our hairdos?

If we examine the culture of the Canaanites, we would find that the Canaanites were literally cutting designs in their hair, much as some do today. Moreover, they were doing so for religious purposes. Thus we discover that, most likely, God's instructions concerning our hair were intended to prevent us from acting like the Canaanites or practicing their religion. Hence, in the course of our research, we discovered that this teaching actually has very little to do with the *peyot,* or sidecurls, worn by many religious Jewish men.

3. Is this passage quoted in the Brit Hadasha?

This is very important. If the passage under question is mentioned in the Brit Chadasha, we may be able to learn at least two possible things from its usage there. First, we may be able to see how this passage was understood by others who lived closer than we to the time it was written. Second, we may be able to learn how that teaching was practiced by those who were part of that same essential culture.

One of the best examples we can think of is the passage in Deuteronomy, "man shall not live by bread alone, but by every word that proceeds from the mouth of God." This verse is quoted in Matthew 4. Here we are afforded an opportunity to see how the Messiah Himself understood and applied this verse from the Torah.

4. How was this teaching practiced in ancient Israel?

Determining how the ancient Israelites understood a teaching in the Torah can help us in our understanding of that passage. For example, it is beneficial to know that the orthodox Jewish practice of "wrapping tefillin" (binding a box containing portions of Torah to one's forehead and arm during prayer, as Deuteronomy 6 apparently teaches) was practiced by those who lived in the Second Temple period. We have ample evidence of this from both archaeological and literary sources. If Israel has been following an instruction of the Torah for centuries, perhaps we too might benefit from practicing it as they do, so long as we do not contradict the written Word.

5. How do Jewish people practice this teaching today?

Jewish practice and interpretation of the Torah began centuries ago—in many cases even before the time of Yeshua. Although we may not believe in the authority of the oral law, it nevertheless contains much that is useful for us today (such as an incredibly insightful periodic interpretation of the Torah). It is helpful for us, therefore, to read some of the best of the modern Jewish commentators (at least those of both the *Rishonim* and *Acharonim*), because in them we may find accurate interpretations of the most difficult passages of the Torah.

Moreover, it can also be helpful to examine some of the rabbinic applications of the Torah, as some of these *halachic* teachings might shed some light for us on a given passage.

6. What Torah picture is painted by the passage?

At first glance, the concept of "Torah pictures" may seem similar to that of "types" so often employed by Bible teachers. But we're talking about something a little different. A Torah picture answers the question, "What does this instruction teach us about the person and work of Yeshua?" In addition, we can also ask, "What does this Torah teaching illustrate concerning our identity in Messiah?"

For example, we find a wonderful Torah picture in the teaching concerning purity and impurity, *tamei* and *tahor.* Why did God declare some things tamei and others tahor?

These words are often translated "unclean" or "clean," respectively. Are such objects or people really "dirty" or "clean"? Is this the intended meaning?

The more we study the matter, the more a whole new universe of pictures opens up for us. Bearing in mind our prior warnings against spiritualization, we nevertheless can see that the concepts of tamei and tahor aptly illustrate our transformation from a state of uncleanness to one of being able to approach God's throne of grace. Yeshua has made us new creations—saints instead of sinners, no longer tahor but tamei. Torah pictures can illustrate these truths and more.

How to Teach the Torah

Having briefly laid out the standard hermeneutical rules for understanding the Torah, we can now introduce a method which should be useful both for organizing your own study and also in presenting it to others.

The key word above is *organize*. What we are about to unfold for you is nothing new. We learned this method from fine Bible teachers years ago, and have taught it to many others since then.

A. Apply all rules of interpretation continually.

Make sure that your interpretation of the Torah passage is as accurate as possible at each step along the way. You can do this by continually applying all of the hermeneutical rules which we have outlined for you above, no matter where you are in your process of preparing a Torah lesson.

Here is a short and simple outline to use when completing your study of a Torah section.

First ask, "What does the passage *say?*"

Next ask, "What does it *mean?*"

Finally, ask, "What does it mean to *me?*"

As stated above, the first part of this three-point outline deals with the *observation* stage. Accurate observation of the details and grammar of a passage should always be in progress, in order to ensure that we know exactly what the text is really saying.

After we are satisfied with our knowledge of the facts of the passage, we can begin to determine what they mean. Technically, this is the *interpretation* stage. The facts determine the meaning, not the other way around!

Finally, when we feel we understand the intent of the passage, based on a careful observation of the facts, then—and only then—may we begin to query, "What does this passage have for me?" This is the *application* stage.

B. Determine the organization of the passage.

Yes, you read that statement correctly! Every passage of the Bible, including the Torah, has some kind of an organization. Your job is to ascertain as best you can the *author's* main point and how he developed it. (Of course, this cannot be accomplished without going through the above three-point plan.) As you begin to figure out the organization or logical development of the passage, begin to reflect that organization in your own outline, proceeding as follows:

1. Give the passage a title.

The title of the passage must be derived from its contents, and must reflect your understanding of the author's intent. In other words, do not force your own ideas onto the passage. Deal only with the true contents of the section of Torah you are studying.

The title you choose for the section may be derived from the actual words of the text, or may be put into your own words—as long as your words constitute an accurate paraphrase of the contents of that section. Remember that the title is really the topic statement of the passage. It is a short, crisp summary of the contents of the section you are studying.

Let us work with an actual example, Exodus 6:2–9. The literary context seems to indicate that this is a somewhat self-defined unit of Torah. The main contents indicate that God is speaking to Moshe concerning His plans for Israel. We can even determine an outline from this passage based on the verbs used. In fact, in verse 7, the fourth verb in the first person singular is a verb that is often used in the Hebrew Bible to describe a man's desire to take a woman for his wife. Based on that fact which I observed, we can therefore give this section a title something like this: "God's Wedding Plans." This title reflects God's intent as revealed in these verses.

2. Outline the passage.

After your section of Scripture is given a title, determine how it develops this theme. *Let the passage generate its own outline.* Do not force an outline onto it. Let the text speak for itself, no matter what it appears to be saying.

There are various ways of creating an outline. You can summarize the main points of logical development in your own words; choose key words from the passage; or choose key sentences from the passage. Let us return to our example.

Exodus 6:2–9, "God's Wedding Plans"

   I.   God Promises to Separate His Bride—"I will bring you out."

   II. God Promises to Deliver His Bride—"I will deliver you."

  III. God Promises to Redeem His Bride—"I will redeem you."

  IV. God Promises to Marry His Bride—"I will take you."

   V.   God Promises a Home for His Bride—"I will bring you."

Can you see how the passage determined both title and outline for this study? In this case I used the main verbs to form the outline. You may want to use the same method or a different one, depending on your text.

3. Develop your outline.

The main body of your study will be developed around your outline. Show how each part of the passage is connected to the outline. Bring in any appropriate Hebrew word studies which will clarify the meaning of the passage. Share any vital historical, cultural, geographical, or religious background information which sheds light on the passage. But work around the basic outline. After studying awhile, you may find that the outline needs to be altered. This is fine if the change is based on your study, and not on your desire to make the passage say something it doesn't.

4. Teach the passage from your outline.

Your title and outline become the main tools by which you can communicate the passage to others. Teaching from an outline usually helps people follow you more easily. In addition, using the outline will force you to stick to the passage and not wander off on a tangent.

5. Teach by asking questions.

One of the best ways to teach a Torah passage, especially if you are teaching a small group, is to use study questions. The best are those which utilize the six discovery words mentioned earlier in this section: *who, what, where, when, how,* and *why.* Your teaching can turn into a great "educated discussion" if you simply turn the points you discovered into questions for the whole group.

For example, you may want your study group to begin by answering the question, "What is the main point of this passage—in your own words?" You have simply turned your title from a statement into a question.

Next you might say, "Let us see how this theme is developed in our Torah section. What is the first promise that God makes concerning Israel in Exodus 6:6?" Here you have communicated to the group your discovery that God makes promises to Israel in the study passage. Now they can discover *for themselves* what these promises are by looking for the promises instead of relying on you to tell them. Finally, practice the art of asking good questions to help your group in developing the passage.

You will need to keep several key points in mind when doing this type of teaching from the Torah. First, you cannot succeed unless you yourself have thoroughly studied the passage. Second, it is important for the individual personal growth of your students that they learn to ask questions from the Torah (or any biblical passage) and find the answers for themselves. They will learn to ask the best questions as you show them how, and their retention rate will be higher than if you simply lectured to them. Finally, never ask the group a question for which a "yes" or "no" may be given as the answer.

6. A word about commentaries and other books

Some people simply will not use commentaries or study aids when studying the Bible. They say they want God to teach them, not man. The problem with this statement is that God has specifically blessed certain people in the body of Messiah with the gift of teaching. We are not disputing the fact that people can discover wonderful things in the Torah by themselves. But God's usual method is to gift certain people who can, in turn, teach others the truths of His Word. Hence, we all need to rely on the God-gifted Torah teachers whom the Holy One places in our path.

Furthermore, we must also realize that most commentaries were originally sermons or verbal teachings before they appeared in print. If we are willing to ask another person his or her opinion about a given passage in the Bible, we should be willing to consult a commentary. There is no difference, other than the fact that one is a verbal opinion about the Torah and the other is written.

We are not islands unto ourselves. We are members of the body of Messiah, each equipped with certain areas of understanding which, when combined, help bring to all of us a more complete understanding of the Bible. Thus, do not throw away all the books and say you will just study the Bible. God never meant for His people to function like that.

(See Appendix C for a list of some of our favorite Torah commentaries and study aids.)

C. Do what the Torah says.

Studying the Torah was not meant to be an end in itself; the book was designed to be practiced, lived out. The Torah teacher who does not encourage his students to practice what the Torah says is not accurately teaching the Torah! Moreover, the teacher who does not attempt to live it out himself is setting the wrong kind of example for his students.

Perhaps the best illustration of this comes from Acts 21, examined earlier in this book. Sha'ul of Tarsus had acquired a reputation for being a fine teacher of the Torah. When the leadership of the Messianic community heard rumors that he was teaching others not to follow the Torah, they required him to do something commanded in the Torah—not merely to say something—in order to prove those rumors false. Of course, being the great Torah teacher that he was, he graciously complied with their request.

A Unique Torah Study Aid: The Torah Club

The primary goal of the publishers of this book is to help people study the Torah and respond to it in their everyday lives. To this end, they have developed a unique system designed to help people in their own individual or group Torah study. It is called the First Fruits of Zion *Torah Club*.

The *Torah Club* utilizes the principles outlined above to produce commentaries on the weekly Torah portions in both audiocassette and print formats. The audio version "eavesdrops" on a dialogue between two Messianic rabbis as they discuss difficult issues relating to each parasha. The written commentary includes an expositional outline of the body of the portion built on a study of the Hebrew text, as well as the historical, cultural and religious backgrounds of the text. This outline enables the student to teach the passage to a group or use it as a sermon. At the end of each week's study are notes designed to help further illuminate the meaning of the text. A list of study questions is also furnished which can facilitate deeper individual meditation, as well as form the basis for a group study.

In short, the *Torah Club* attempts to model the study method discussed above. Moreover, it also furnishes the student with a rich commentary on each weekly Torah portion from a Messianic Jewish viewpoint. This means that the commentators utilize the insights and research of the best of the Jewish sages as well as evangelical scholars in analyzing each passage.

The *Torah Club* comes in two volumes, with a third currently in the works. The first volume is designed to introduce the reader to the world of Jewish thought, as well as lay a foundation for the study of Torah. The second approaches each weekly portion with the goal of discovering what it reveals of the person and work of Yeshua the Messiah. Volume Three will explore insights gleaned from the Haftarah (portions from the Prophets). A *Children's Torah Club* is available as well, which contains games and activities designed to help youngsters begin their own journey through the Scriptures.

Appendix B
The Weekly Torah Readings

It is extremely rewarding to read through the Torah (as well as the rest of the Bible!) on a regular basis. You can follow any scheme of regular readings you want. But, as the saying goes, "Why reinvent the wheel?" It would be difficult to improve on the weekly Torah reading plan which the Jewish people have followed for centuries.

We do not know when the traditional plan of readings began. Josephus, writing in the latter half of the first century, tells us that the Jewish people have had a regular Torah reading cycle since ancient times (*Apion* 2:175). However, we do know that from the time of the late Second Temple period a rather fixed schedule was in place in the synagogues. The Talmud provides us with the evidence for this, as does the Brit Chadasha (cf. Acts 15:21).

The earliest reference to a fixed cycle of consecutive readings of the Torah is in *B.T. Megillah 29b*. Here we see that in

Israel there was a three-year reading cycle. In Babylon and elsewhere in the diaspora, there was a one-year reading cycle consisting of 54 different portions. The three-year cycle continued to be used in certain places, at least up until the 1200s, as the Rambam attests. However, since at least Talmudic times (200–500 CE), the usual custom has been to read the Torah in a year.

Following a one-year cycle of consecutive readings, the ancient practice of dividing the Torah into 54 portions is still followed. A portion is called a *parasha* or a *sidra*. (The plural would be *parashiot* and *sedarim*, respectively.) There are occasions when two portions are combined on one Shabbat in order to fit all 54 parashiot into one year.

Each portion is given a Hebrew name derived from the first significant word in that parasha. In the case of the first portion of each book, the name given is the same as the Hebrew title of the book. For example, the first portion in Genesis is called "Bereshit." (Bereshit is also the Hebrew title for the Book of Genesis.)

We have included a list of the weekly portions following a one-year Torah reading cycle. The actual reading dates are not listed, however, as these vary from year to year according to the Hebrew calendar. The reading dates in Israel also differ from those in the diaspora; this is because certain Holy Days which Israel celebrates for one day are extended elsewhere to two. First Fruits of Zion publishes a calendar that includes each week's Torah portion along with its corresponding diaspora date. Calendars can also be found in most Jewish bookstores.

Each Shabbat, a different Torah portion is read (in consecutive order) and followed by a corresponding reading from one of the prophetic books. Again, the origin of the particular portions from the Prophets, as well as the custom of reading from them, is very obscure. However, we know from Luke

4:17 that it was the common practice to do so, at least in the late Second Temple period.

The reading from the Prophets is called the *Haftarah* reading. Haftarah means "completion." The idea is that the reading of the Prophets completes the Torah reading. We have provided you with the weekly Haftarah readings which go along with the Torah readings. You may note that some of these readings come from historical books such as Kings or Samuel. This is because, in the Jewish division of the Tenach (the Older Testament), these historical books are considered part of the prophetic books.

As you read through the Torah portions, you will want to keep several things in mind. First, realize that if you follow the traditional reading schedule, there are millions of Jewish people doing the same thing you are doing at the same time. That is a lot of Bible reading taking place! In many synagogues, there are study groups where the weekly parasha is read and studied. They sometimes meet on Shabbat or during the weekdays. Your study would be greatly enhanced by attending such a group.

Second, remember that it is God's Word that you are studying. It is a blessing to read and study it. Traditional Jewish people have developed blessings for almost every experience in life, demonstrating their thankfulness to the Holy One for each part of their life. It is the same with reading the Bible. Accordingly, it is customary to bless God before and after the reading of the Torah and the Haftarah.

We have included the traditional blessings here. They are in English, transliterated Hebrew, and Hebrew. Please note not only the beauty of these blessings, but also the truth they contain. They accurately express what the new creation believes about the God who has revealed Himself in the Scriptures!

If you are involved in a group study, the leader could recite the blessings on behalf of the whole group. If you want more liturgical information about the typical Torah reading service in the synagogue, you can read it in any *Siddur* (prayer book).

Blessing Before the Torah Is Read

Blessed are You, O Lord our God, King of the Universe, who selected us from all the peoples and gave us His Torah. Blessed are You, O Lord, the Giver of the Torah. Amen.

Baruch atah Adonai eloheinu melech ha-olam, asher bachar banu mikol ha-amim, v'natan lanu et Torato. Baruch atah Adonai, notein haTorah. Amen.

בָּרוּךְ אַתָּה, יהוה אֱלֹהֵינוּ, מֶלֶךְ הָעוֹלָם,
אֲשֶׁר בָּחַר־בָּנוּ מִכָּל־הָעַמִּים וְנָתַן־לָנוּ אֶת־תּוֹרָתוֹ;
בָּרוּךְ אַתָּה, יהוה, נוֹתֵן הַתּוֹרָה !

Blessing After the Torah Has Been Read

Blessed are You, O Lord our God, King of the Universe, who gave us the Torah of truth and planted everlasting life within us. Blessed are You, O Lord, the Giver of the Torah. Amen.

Baruch atah Adonai eloheinu melech ha-olam, asher natan lanu Torat emet, v'chayei olam nata b'tocheinu. Baruch atah Adonai, notein haTorah. Amen.

בָּרוּךְ אַתָּה, יהוה אֱלֹהֵינוּ, מֶלֶךְ הָעוֹלָם,
אֲשֶׁר נָתַן־לָנוּ תּוֹרַת־אֱמֶת, וְחַיֵּי עוֹלָם נָטַע בְּתוֹכֵנוּ;
בָּרוּךְ אַתָּה, יהוה, נוֹתֵן הַתּוֹרָה !

Blessing Before Reading the Haftarah

Blessed are You, O Lord our God, King of the Universe, who has chosen good prophets and was pleased with their words that are stated in truth. Blessed are You, O Lord, who chooses the Torah; Moshe, His servant; Israel, His nation; and the prophets of truth and righteousness. Amen.

Baruch atah Adonai eloheinu melech ha-olam, asher bachar binvi'im tovim, vratza b'divreihem ha-ne'emarim b'emet. Baruch atah Adonai habocher baTorah, uv'Moshe avdo, uv'Yisrael amo, uvin'viei ha-emet v'hatzedek. Amen.

בָּרוּךְ אַתָּה, יהוה אֱלֹהֵינוּ, מֶלֶךְ הָעוֹלָם,
אֲשֶׁר בָּחַר בִּנְבִיאִים טוֹבִים, וְרָצָה בְּדִבְרֵיהֶם הַנֶּאֱמָרִים בֶּאֱמֶת.
בָּרוּךְ אַתָּה, יהוה, הַבּוֹחֵר בַּתּוֹרָה,
וּבְמֹשֶׁה עַבְדּוֹ וּבְיִשְׂרָאֵל עַמּוֹ, וּבִנְבִיאֵי הָאֱמֶת וְהַצֶּדֶק !

Blessing After the Haftarah Has Been Read

(The blessing which is usually said is a rather lengthy one, and includes other things besides a blessing for the Prophets. Therefore, we will include here only the first paragraph, without a transliteration or the Hebrew.)

Blessed are You, O Lord our God, King of the Universe, Rock of all the worlds, righteous throughout all generations, O faithful God, who says and does, who speaks and fulfills, all of whose words are true and just. Faithful are You, O Lord our God, and faithful are Your words. Not one of Your promises will remain unfulfilled, for You are a faithful and merciful King. Blessed are You, the God who is faithful in all His words.

The annual Torah and Haftarah reading schedule is as follows:

Bereshit "In the beginning"

Torah reading: Genesis 1:1–6:8
Haftarah reading: Isaiah 42:5–43:11

Noach "Noah"

Torah reading: Genesis 6:9–11:32
Haftarah reading: Isaiah 54:1–55:5

Lech Lecha "Go out"

Torah reading: Genesis 12:1–17:27
Haftarah reading: Isaiah 40:27–41:16

Vayera "And appeared"

Torah reading: Genesis 18:1–22:24
Haftarah reading: II Kings 4:1–37

Chayei Sarah "And Sarah's life"

Torah reading: Genesis 23:1–25:18
Haftarah reading: I Kings 1:1–31

Toldot "Generations"

Torah reading: Genesis 25:19–28:9
Haftarah reading: Malachi 1:1–2:7

Vayetze "And went out"

Torah reading: Genesis 28:10–32:3
Haftarah reading: Hosea 12:13–14:10

Vayishlach "And he sent"

Torah reading: Genesis 32:4–36:43
Haftarah reading: Hosea 11:7–12:12

Vayeshev "And he dwelt"

Torah reading: Genesis 37:1–40:23
Haftarah reading: Amos 2:6–3:8

Miketz "At the end"

Torah reading: Genesis 41:1–44:17
Haftarah reading: I Kings 3:15–4:1

Vayigash "And approached"

Torah reading: Genesis 44:18–47:27
Haftarah reading: Ezekiel 37:15–28

Vayechi "And he lived"

Torah reading: Genesis 47:28–50:26
Haftarah reading: I Kings 2:1–12

Shemot "Names"

Torah reading: Exodus 1:1–6:1
Haftarah reading: Isaiah 27:6–28:13; 29:22–23

Va'eira "And I appeared"

Torah reading: Exodus 6:2–9:35
Haftarah reading: Ezekiel 28:25–29:21

Bo "Come"

Torah reading: Exodus 10:1–13:16
Haftarah reading: Jeremiah 46:13–28

Beshalach "When he sent"

Torah reading: Exodus 13:17–17:16
Haftarah reading: Judges 4:4–5:31

Yitro "Jethro"

Torah reading: Exodus 18:1–20:23
Haftarah reading: Isaiah 6:1–7:6, 9:5–6

Mishpatim "Judgments"

Torah reading: Exodus 21:1–24:18
Haftarah reading: Jeremiah 34:8–22; 33:25–26

Terumah "Heave offering"

Torah reading: Exodus 25:1–27:19
Haftarah reading: I Kings 5:26–6:13

Tetzaveh "You shall command"

Torah reading: Exodus 27:20–30:10
Haftarah reading: Ezekiel 43:10–27

Ki Thissa "When you number"

Torah reading: Exodus 30:11–34:35
Haftarah reading: I Kings 18:1–39

Vayachel "And assembled"

Torah reading: Exodus 35:1–38:20
Haftarah reading: I Kings 7:40–50

Pekudei "Accounts"

Torah reading: Exodus 38:21–40:38
Haftarah reading: I Kings 7:51–8:21

Vayikra "And he called"

Torah reading: Leviticus 1:1–5:26
Haftarah reading: Isaiah 43:21–44:23

Tzav "Command"

Torah reading: Leviticus 6:1–8:36
Haftarah reading: Jeremiah 7:21–8:3; 9:22–23

Shemini "Eighth"

Torah reading: Leviticus 9:1–11:47
Haftarah reading: II Samuel 6:1–7:17

Tazria "Conceived"

Torah reading: Leviticus 12:1–13:59
Haftarah reading: II Kings 4:42–5:19

Metzora "Leper"

Torah reading: Leviticus 14:1–15:33
Haftarah reading: II Kings 7:3–20

Acharei Mot "After the death"

Torah reading: Leviticus 16:1–18:30
Haftarah reading: Ezekiel 22:1–19

Kedoshim "Holy"

Torah reading: Leviticus 19:1–20:27
Haftarah reading: Amos 9:7–15

Emor "Say"

Torah reading: Leviticus 21:1–24:23
Haftarah reading: Ezekiel 44:15–31

Behar "On Mount Sinai"

Torah reading: Leviticus 25:1–26:2
Haftarah reading: Jeremiah 32:6–27

Bechukotai "In My statutes"

Torah reading: Leviticus 26:3–27:34
Haftarah reading: Jeremiah 16:19–17:14

Bemidbar "In the wilderness"

Torah reading: Numbers 1:1–4:20
Haftarah reading: Hosea 2:1–22

Naso "Make an accounting"

Torah reading: Numbers 4:21–7:89
Haftarah reading: Judges 13:2–25

Beha'alotcha "When you set up"

Torah reading: Numbers 8:1–12:16
Haftarah reading: Zechariah 2:14–4:7

Shlach "Send thou"

Torah reading: Numbers 13:1–15:41
Haftarah reading: Joshua 2:1–24

Korach "Korah"

Torah reading: Numbers 16:1–18:32
Haftarah reading: I Samuel 11:14–12:22

Chukat "Statute"

Torah reading: Numbers 19:1–22:1
Haftarah reading: Judges 11:1–33

Balak "Balak"

Torah reading: Numbers 22:2–25:9
Haftarah reading: Micah 5:6–6:8

Pinchas "Phineas"

Torah reading: Numbers 25:10–30:1
Haftarah reading: I Kings 18:46–19:21

Matot "Tribes"

Torah reading: Numbers 30:2–32:42
Haftarah reading: Jeremiah 1:1–2:3

Massei "Journeys"

Torah reading: Numbers 33:1–36:13
Haftarah reading: Jeremiah 2:4–28; 3:4

Devarim "Words"

Torah reading: Deuteronomy 1:1–3:22
Haftarah reading: Isaiah 1:1–27

Va'etchanan "And I besought"

Torah reading: Deuteronomy 3:23–7:11
Haftarah reading: Isaiah 40:1–26

Ekev "Because"

Torah reading: Deuteronomy 7:12–11:25
Haftarah reading: Isaiah 49:14–51:3

Re'eh "Behold"

Torah reading: Deuteronomy 11:26–16:17
Haftarah reading: Isaiah 54:11–55:5

Shoftim "Judges"

Torah reading: Deuteronomy 16:18–21:9
Haftarah reading: Isaiah 51:12–52:12

Ki Tetze "When you go"

Torah reading: Deuteronomy 21:10–25:19
Haftarah reading: Isaiah 54:1–10

Ki Tavo "When you come"

Torah reading: Deuteronomy 26:1–29:8
Haftarah reading: Isaiah 60:1–22

Nitzavim "You are standing"

Torah reading: Deuteronomy 29:9–30:20
Haftarah reading: Isaiah 61:10–63:9

Vayelech "And he went"

Torah reading: Deuteronomy 31:1–30
Haftarah reading: Isaiah 55:6–56:8

Haazinu "Give ear"

Torah reading: Deuteronomy 32:1–52
Haftarah reading: II Samuel 22:1–51

Vezot Haberachah "And this is the blessing"

Torah reading: Deuteronomy 33:1–34:12
Haftarah reading: Joshua 1:1–18

Appendix C
Torah Study Aids

In this section we would like to familiarize you with the world of Torah commentaries. If you are a novice in this area, it may help to remember that there is very little difference between reading a Bible commentary and listening to a sermon. In fact, many commentaries were originally sermons themselves! We will mention just a few of those which we have found most helpful in our Torah study.

From the Evangelical World

In our studies in the Torah, we prefer those commentaries that provide the most accurate and detailed historical background information of the times in which the Torah was written. Thus, the books we recommend are as follows:

1. *The Tyndale Old Testament Commentary Series*. This includes volumes by Derek Kidner on Genesis, R. Alan Cole

on Exodus, R. K. Harrison on Leviticus, Gordon J. Wenham on Numbers, and J. A. Thompson on Deuteronomy.

2. *The New International Commentary on the Old Testament*. These books include: Genesis chapters 1–17, by Victor Hamilton, Leviticus by Gordon J. Wenham, Numbers by Timothy R. Ashley, and Deuteronomy by P. C. Craigie. As far as we know, the commentary on Exodus has not yet been published.

3. The *Keil and Delitsch* commentaries on the Old Testament are also great, especially if you like to work in the Hebrew.

4. Since the first edition of *Torah Rediscovered* was published, we have found a great trilogy of books on the entire Tenach by the distinguished scholar Walter Kaiser. We highly recommend any of his writing. Regretfully, we have not been able to secure any of these books for our own study of the Torah; hence they are not listed in our bibliography. Ironically enough, it is sometimes very difficult to get the desired biblical resources here in Israel!

5. For those of you who don't feel quite ready for such scholarly works, we highly recommend any commentary produced by *Dr. Louis Goldberg*. To the best of our knowledge, he has only written commentaries on Leviticus and Deuteronomy, both of which are part of Zondervan's "Lamplighter Books" series.

6. As far as we know, they have only produced one commentary on the Torah (Genesis), but any commentary by *Dr. James M. Boice* and *Dr. Leon Morris* is bound to be rich reading with helpful insights.

7. One of our favorite commentaries, produced by the Jewish Publication Society of Philadelphia, is *The JPS Torah Commentary* (affectionately known as "the JPS"). Published in five volumes, the JPS is especially helpful in Hebrew word meanings and historical background material.

8. It can be very instructive to look up the various topics discussed in the Torah. Our favorite place to do this is in *The International Standard Bible Encyclopedia*.

We are sure that there are many excellent Torah commentaries in addition to those mentioned here. We encourage you to find your own favorites!

Jewish Commentaries

Naturally, the oldest commentaries on the Torah are written by Jewish scholars. Any student of the Torah should be at least somewhat familiar with the classic Jewish works in this area. The most serious students of the Torah *must* utilize Jewish commentaries!

For those of you who have never swum in the sea of rabbinic literature, you may need a little help getting your feet wet. It can be very tricky if you are not prepared for a different way of thinking. The key to understanding Jewish commentaries is to realize that the rabbis use a different method of interpreting the Bible than most evangelicals. They seek at least four levels of interpreting any given text. The first level begins with the most literal or obvious sense of the words or text. However, that is just a starting point. The goal is to look for the deepest sense of every phrase, word, and even letter in the Hebrew. In order to accomplish this task, there is widespread use of the allegorical method of interpretation. This is employed in cases where little or nothing can be gained from working at the literal or obvious level, enabling each passage to be understood in a symbolic or spiritual sense. As one may imagine, historical backgrounds, while utilized from time to time, actually play a very minor role in ascertaining the ultimate understanding of the text.

One more unique feature of rabbinic interpretation is the use of *gematria*, a system of interpreting biblical text by determining the numerical values of each word. This system is based on the fact that Hebrew letters also have numerical value. These numerical values and the combinations thereof are used to decipher some meanings "behind" the text. However, it is not as simple as this definition makes it sound. Indeed, several books have been published explaining the intricacies of the whole system of gematria. In addition to the different hermeneutical methods used by the rabbis, anyone using Jewish commentaries needs to understand that the Jewish worldview is often drastically different than the "standard" evangelical worldview—if there is one!

Notwithstanding these cultural differences, it is very helpful to read the classic (and sometimes not so classic) Jewish commentaries on the Torah. In some cases, the sages have been given tremendous insights into the biblical text. At other times, however, we are left wondering how they could possibly have come up with a given viewpoint. Hence, we are not suggesting that you should adopt an interpretation just because a rabbi or a sage says it. On the contrary, each interpretation should be scrutinized very carefully! The Jewish commentaries, however, offer a different insight into the Torah. They also may contribute to the history of the interpretation of a given text. Indeed, sometimes (especially when studying the Midrash, Targum, or the Talmud) we are looking at how the sages have understood the Bible well before the time of Yeshua, depending on whose viewpoint we are reading. That can sometimes be extremely helpful in studying the Bible, especially the Torah. Moreover, it is exciting to learn how the Jewish sages understood particular passages in an era which predated the reactionary interpretations that began to appear after the Christian era.

The following is a very brief annotated bibliography of some of the most important Jewish works providing commentary on the Torah.

1. *The Talmud* (both Babylonian and Jerusalem Talmuds). This is a huge collection of oral law, first written down around the year 500 CE. Some of its contents, however, reflect an oral tradition dating from a time well before the arrival of Yeshua. Much of the Talmud consists of legal debates between rabbis. But there is also a great deal of commentary on the Torah. The Soncino Press has an English edition with some notes and several kinds of indexes. We understand that ArtScroll also has an English edition with more elaborate explanatory notes.

2. *The Mishnah*. This is the first of the two sections of the Talmud, the other being the Gemarah (a much longer section which elaborates on the Mishnah). This is oral law, so it contains many legal sections. But, like the Talmud, it contains many comments on the Torah as well. It is much easier to purchase than the Talmud. The most popular one-volume edition of the Mishnah is the one translated by Herbert Danby.

3. *The Midrash Rabbah* is specifically a commentary. There are several midrashim from ancient times. But the Midrash Rabbah is the most popular one accessible in English. It is a multi-volume set of commentaries on the Torah and the *Megilot* (Song of Solomon, Ruth, Lamentations, Ecclesiastes, and Esther). This is a classic example of the allegorical method of interpretation. The Midrash Rabbah was written sometime between 300 and 900 CE.

4. *Aramaic Targums* are paraphrases and translations of the Hebrew Scriptures (some now in English) dating from sometime in the late Second Temple period. They provide important insight into how a Torah text was understood during that time period, some of which predated Yeshua's time.

5. There are various "Torah Study Bibles" circulating in the Jewish world. Such a volume is called a *Chumash*, taken from the Hebrew word for "five." It refers to the Five Books of

Moshe, the Torah. These *Chumashim* contain the Torah in both the English and Hebrew texts. Sometimes they also offer Targum Onkelos in Aramaic. The text is arranged according to the weekly Torah portions. Each portion is followed by the Haftarah, or weekly reading of the Prophets, which has been chosen to correspond to the Torah reading. Explanatory notes are also provided.

Our favorite Chumash is called *The Pentateuch and Haftarahs*, edited by Rabbi J. H. Hertz. He is the most literal and offers many excellent historical notes. There are other popular volumes to choose from as well, such as the ArtScroll Chumash and another which is edited by Rabbi S. R. Hirsch. All three can easily be purchased (as can all of these books) in any Jewish religious bookstore.

The above works are the best ways to get Jewish comments on any given Torah passage. There are also individual commentaries on the Torah written by some famous and important sages. Here are some of them:

1. **Rashi.** The most respected Jewish commentator, he wrote a commentary on the Torah sometime during the 1000s. His brevity is deceiving. Every Jewish student knows about Rashi, called by one scholar "the prince of Jewish Bible commentators."

2. **Rambam.** Rabbi Moshe ben Maimon (Maimonides) wrote a highly respected commentary on the Torah sometime in the 1100s. He was also a world-famous medical doctor!

3. **Ramban.** As in the case of Rashi and Rambam, "Ramban" is not this commentator's given name, but an acronym derived from the first letters of his personal names. Writing in the 1200s, Ramban was sometimes at odds with Rambam (Moshe ben Nachman). His commentary is flavored with the Kabbalah (mystical writings) and may also reflect something of his famed debates with Christian theologians.

4. **Ibn Ezra, Abravanel, and Sforno** are all very popular Torah commentators from the early Renaissance period in Europe.

5. **Rav Kook.** The first Chief Rabbi of (then) Palestine is someone to take very seriously in your Torah study.

6. **Nechama Leibowitz.** It is highly unusual to have a woman Bible commentator respected and approved by the Orthodox Jewish world. Leibowitz's multi-volume commentary on the Torah does not comment on every verse, but it does raise many helpful questions and provides many extremely insightful remarks on the issues from the Torah that she does discuss. Leibowitz is one of our favorite Torah commentators.

7. Last, but not least, is a great multi-volume Torah commentary by **Rabbi Elie Munk.** Munk provides a great summary of what many of the classic sages such as Rashi and Rambam say about a given text. He attempts to comment on every verse.

8. While not a commentary, the *Encyclopedia Judaica* has nevertheless always proven helpful for background information related to Jewish studies and Jewish Torah interpretation.

Messianic Jewish Commentaries

For reasons unknown to us, there are very few Torah commentaries written by Jewish believers, particularly those who are favorable toward the Torah lifestyle.

As mentioned earlier, **Dr. Louis Goldberg** has authored credible works on Leviticus and Deuteronomy which are highly useful as reference tools.

First Fruits of Zion Ministry has also produced several exhaustive commentaries on the weekly Torah portions. For further details, see Appendix A.

Scripture Index

Acts

Acts 15	70, 71, 73, 146
Acts 15:9	70
Acts 15:19–21	71
Acts 15:19–20	72
Acts 15:21	72
Acts 21	20, 71, 117-119, 120, 130
Acts 21:15-26	20
Acts 21:17–26	119
Acts 21:20ff	118, 129
Acts 21:21	61
Acts 21:23–26	119
Acts 21:26	61

Corinthians

I Corinthians 1	44
I Corinthians 5:17	44
I Corinthians 12:2	73
II Corinthians 4:7	86, 148
II Corinthians 5:21	44, 85

Deuteronomy

Deuteronomy 1:1–5	10
Deuteronomy 1:6–4:49	10
Deuteronomy 3:25	102
Deuteronomy 4	73
Deuteronomy 4:5–8	26, 67
Deuteronomy 5:1–26:19	10
Deuteronomy 12	25
Deuteronomy 17:14–20	99
Deuteronomy 17:8–13	97
Deuteronomy 27–30	10
Deuteronomy 29:1	8
Deuteronomy 30:11–14	109, 110
Deuteronomy 30:14–15	37
Deuteronomy 30:19	10, 149
Deuteronomy 30:19–20	27
Deuteronomy 31:1–8	10
Deuteronomy 31:9–13	10
Deuteronomy 32:47	39, 145

Ephesians

Ephesians 1:4	44
Ephesians 2	146
Ephesians 2:5	44
Ephesians 2:6	44
Ephesians 2:10	44
Ephesians 2:11–13	73, 74

Exodus

Exodus 6	12
Exodus 6:6–7	11
Exodus 19:5–7	12
Exodus 19:9	12
Exodus 19ff	30
Exodus 20	12
Exodus 31:12–17	13
Exodus 31:18	12
Exodus 34:27	8

Ezekiel

Ezekiel 47	75

Glossary

We have chosen to use the Jewish form of certain names and phrases in this book for specific reasons. Foremost among these is to maintain a Jewish sensibility so that the book may be "user friendly" for Jewish readers. We have provided this glossary for those readers unfamiliar with Jewish terminology.

It is sometimes difficult to transliterate words from one language to another. Accordingly, we have encountered certain problems in transliterating some words from Hebrew or Greek into English; hence, we have listed variant spellings in cases where more than one rendering is possible.

ז״ל—This Hebrew abbreviation is one of several commonly used to follow the name of the deceased. The two Hebrew words which comprise this abbreviation mean, "May the memory of this person be for a blessing."

BCE, CE—This is the Jewish way of dating or reckoning the centuries. BCE = Before the Common Era (BC), and CE = Common Era (AD). By using these terms we are in no way attempting to diminish the centrality of Yeshua in our lives, or to deprive Him of His due honor. We are merely endeavoring to be sensitive to Jewish feelings.

Brit Chadasha—Literally, "New Covenant." For use in this book, it refers to the New Testament.

Chukim—Hebrew for "statutes."

Chumash—The first Five Books of the Bible, Genesis through Deuteronomy. The term is derived from the Hebrew word for "five."

Chuppah—A canopy in a Jewish wedding under which the wedding party stands during the service.

Church fathers—The Christian scholars and leaders who preached and wrote between approximately 100 to 450 CE.

Counting the Days—This is a period of time specified by Leviticus 23, falling between Pesach and Shavuot. We are merely told to "count the days."

First Jewish Revolt—The First Jewish Revolt was a Jewish rebellion against Roman rule occurring between the years 66–73 CE. The results were a defeat for the Jews and the total destruction of the Temple in Jerusalem.

Gemarah—"Completion." This is the second and longer of the two pieces of literature which comprise the Talmud. The Gemarah completes the Mishnah by functioning as its commentary.

Haftarah—To complement the Torah portions, the Prophets and the Writings have also been divided into weekly readings and are read following the Torah portion.

Halacha—Derived from the Hebrew word meaning "walk," this is the way one is to walk out or live one's life, based on the teachings of both written and oral Torah. In a sense, halachic Judaism is rabbinic or traditional Judaism. A halacha is also a specific legal decision in a given area of life which a person is to follow.

Hebrew names for the books of the Torah:

Hebrew Title	Literal Translation	English Title
Bereshit	In the Beginning	Genesis
Shemot	Names	Exodus
Vayikra	And He Called	Leviticus
Bemidbar	In the Wilderness	Numbers
Devarim	Words	Deuteronomy

Ketubah—A written Jewish marriage contract.

Kosher—Kosher means "fit to be eaten according to Jewish dietary laws." The noun derived from it is *kashrut*, the system of Jewish dietary laws.

Maimonides (Rambam)—One of the most respected sages in Judaism, Rabbi Moshe ben Maimon (his complete Hebrew name) lived in the 1100s. He was an authority on the Torah and Jewish law. Born in Spain, and a resident of Israel for a short time, Maimonides lived out his days as the court physician for the sultan in Egypt. He wrote several very important works, but is perhaps best known for his *Mishneh Torah*.

Megila, Megilot (plural)—A scroll of one of the following Five Books of the Bible: Esther, Song of Solomon, Ruth, Lamentations, and Ecclesiastes.

Mezuzah—Mezuzah literally means "doorpost." It refers to the small parchment of Scripture which the Torah commands to be placed on the doorpost of our houses.

Midrash—1) A method of interpreting the Tenach, stressing the allegorical method of interpretation. It also is a homiletic way of looking at a biblical text, as opposed to a scholarly or literal approach. 2) The name of certain specific collections of commentaries which have employed the midrashic method of interpretation. The best known is called the *Midrash Rabbah*, which is a commentary on the entire Torah plus the five megilot. Although compiled sometime between the fourth and fifth centuries CE, this Midrash includes some material from Yeshua's time and even before.

Mikvah—A ritual immersion pool.

Mishkan—The Tabernacle.

Mishnah—This is an authoritative collection of oral Torah. It was compiled by Rabbi Yehudah haNasi (Rabbi Judah the Prince) around the year 200 CE. The Mishnah also comprises the smaller of the two pieces of writing that make up the Talmud.

Mishpatim—Hebrew for "judgments."

Mitzvah, mitzvot (plural)—A commandment.

Mo'ed, mo'adim (plural)—Literally, "appointed time." A mo'ed is a Holy Day, either a feast or a fast. A list of the mo'adim is found in chapter 23 of Leviticus.

Moshe—Moses. "Moshe Rabbenu" means "Moses, our teacher."

Nazarenes—Not the church denomination of the same name! The Nazarenes were a group of Jewish believers in Yeshua of unspecified number, from the time of the original apostles to about the early 400s. They were characterized by their exaltation of Yeshua, their acknowledgment of the canonical letters of Sha'ul of Tarsus as Scripture, and their faithfulness to the Torah.

Niddah—The term used to refer to the period of separation between husband and wife during the menstrual period.

Parasha, parashiot (plural)—The weekly Torah portion. Presently, the Torah is divided into 54 portions which are read and studied each week for one year. In ancient times, the

Torah-reading cycle lasted three years. A parasha (portion) is sometimes also called a *sidra*.

Passover, Pesach (Hebrew)—This is the biblically commanded festival in late March or early to mid-April which celebrates the Israelite exodus from slavery in Egypt.

Rabbi Yehudah haNasi—One of the greatest rabbis of all time, credited with compiling the traditional oral teachings into the writing called the Mishnah, circa 200 CE. In the Talmud he is simply referred to as "the Rabbi."

Rabbi Yochanan ben Zakkai—This important sage was one of the pharisaic survivors of the First Jewish Revolt against Rome. He led his disciples from Jerusalem to Yavne (near present day Tel Aviv), where they set out to establish a Judaism which had to exist without a temple. He is often credited with firmly establishing rabbinic Judaism.

Rashi—Generally considered the greatest of Jewish commentators, Rashi lived in France during the 1000s. He authored many works, including a highly regarded commentary on the Torah. His real name was Rabbi Solomon ben Isaac.

Rav Sha'ul—This is a Jewish way of referring to Paul. His Hebrew name was Sha'ul (Saul), and because of his position as a teacher and his training in rabbinic thinking, we have given him the honorary title of "Rav."

Second Jewish Revolt—This was another revolt against the Roman occupation of Israel, taking place between 132–135 CE. This rebellion, led by Simon bar Kochba, also failed. The result was that Jews were no longer permitted anywhere near Jerusalem, whose name was changed by the Romans to Aelia Capitolina. This is technically the *Third* Jewish Revolt, but it was the second that took place in what the Romans called Palestine.

Sefer Torah—The Torah scroll.

Septuagint—The translation of the Hebrew Scriptures into Greek around the year 250 BCE. This was the first known translation of the Tenach. It is often abbreviated to LXX.

Shabbat—The seventh day of the week. In English it is often called the Sabbath, or just Saturday.

Shadchan—A matchmaker, one who helps to arrange Jewish weddings.

Shavuot, Pentecost—The fiftieth day after the Pesach Shabbat. In Judaism, Shavuot is the time when we remember the giving of the Torah on Mount Sinai. It is also a firstfruits holiday. It was on Shavuot that the Spirit of God came upon the early Jewish followers of Yeshua as they were worshiping in the Temple.

Shofar—A ram's horn blown on Rosh Hashanah and other special times.

Shulchan Aruch—The literal meaning of this Hebrew term means "set table." It is the title for a sixteenth-century compendium of halacha, or Jewish law, edited by Joseph Caro.

Succot—The Feast of Tabernacles. This is the biblically commanded festival in late September or early to mid-October when Jewish people live in temporary booths for one week and celebrate the provisions of God.

Tahor—Being in a state of ritual purity. This is a very difficult concept to render into English. The person who is tahor has been removed from a declared state of ritual impurity and declared by God to be free of the vestiges of his or her contact with the realm of sin and/or death. The means of changing the outward state from "tamei" to "tahor" usually involved offering the prescribed sacrifice and purification through water.

Talmid, talmidim (plural)—A "learner," or student. A talmid was really a student who was also a disciple: he did not just learn facts, he also learned life from his teacher.

Talmud—The two-part authoritative compendium of oral law. The main but shorter part is the Mishnah. After each Mishnah is quoted, it is followed by the second, longer part called the Gemarah (a commentary on the Mishnah). There are actually two Talmuds. The more authoritative work is called the Babylonian Talmud, because it was compiled by sages living in or near Babylon sometime around 500 CE. The second, known as the Jerusalem or Palestinian Talmud, was compiled by sages living in what was then called "Palestine" by the Romans—*not* in Jerusalem. The date is also uncertain, but many believe it was finished slightly earlier than the Babylonian Talmud. The English edition by Soncino Press takes up over two feet on a bookshelf!

Tamei—Being in a state of ritual impurity. Like *tahor*, this is a difficult concept to render into English. The person who is tamei has come into contact with the realm of sin and/or death. However, it does not always mean that the person has sinned.

Tenach—An acronym for the Old Testament. T = Torah; N = Neviim (Prophets); Ch = Ketuvim (Writings), the threefold division of the Tenach.

Tzitziot—The "fringes" on a four-cornered garment worn by observant Jewish men.

Ya'acov—The Hebrew for both Jacob and James.

Yeshua—The Hebrew name for Jesus.

Yom Kippur—Day of Atonement.

Yom Teruah—In traditional Judaism, this Holy Day (mo'ed) is known as Rosh Hashanah. Biblically, it is the day set aside for a special blowing of the shofar.

Endnotes

Introduction
[1] David H. Stern, *Messianic Jewish Manifesto* (Jerusalem, 1988), p. 125.

Chapter 1
[2] R. Laird Harris, ed., *Theological Wordbook of the Old Testament* (Chicago, 1980), pp. 403–404.

[3] Rabbi Aryeh Kaplan, *Made in Heaven* (Jerusalem, 1983), p. 99.

[4] David Bivin and Roy Blizzard Jr., *Understanding the Difficult Words of Jesus* (Austin: Center for Judaic-Christian Studies, 1984), p. 154.

[5] Richard Longenecker indicates that one of the names by which the Jewish believers after the Apostles referred to Yeshua was "The Torah" (*haTorah*). See *The Christology of Early Jewish Christianity*, pp. 39–41. See also J. Danielou, *The Theology of Jewish Christianity*.

Chapter 2
[6] William Arndt and J. Wilbur Gingrich, *A Greek-English Lexicon of the New Testament* (Chicago, 1957, 1973), p. 608.

Chapter 3

[7] Rabbi Shlomo Riskin, Ruth: "The Book of Religio-nationality," *The Jerusalem Post*, 23 May 1996, p. 11.

[8] Francis Brown, S. R. Driver, and Charles A. Briggs, *A Hebrew and English Lexicon of the Old Testament* (Oxford, 1907, 1966), pp. 716–720.

Chapter 4

[9] Arnold G. Fruchtenbaum, *Israelology* (Tustin, 1989), p. 643.

[10] A fascinating extrabiblical confirmation of the changing status of the Second Temple after Yeshua's death and resurrection is found in the Talmud (*Yoma 39b*). Here, the sages report that 40 years (one generation) before the Temple was destroyed by the Romans in 70 CE, certain strange phenomena occurred in the Temple which indicated that atonement was not accepted by God on Yom Kippur. This corroborates beautifully with the account in the Gospels that the curtain which separated the Holy of Holies from the Holy Place was torn upon the moment of Yeshua's death, indicating that there was now free access into the most intimate place with God through the atonement accomplished by the Messiah.

[11] John F. Walvoord, ed. *Lewis Sperry Chafer Systematic Theology* vol. II "Abridged Edition" (Wheaton, 1988), II 414.

[12] Rabbi Yechiel Eckstein, *What You Should Know About Jews and Judaism* (Waco, 1984), p. 25.

[13] Walvoord, p. 415.

[14] Ray A. Pritz, *Nazarene Jewish Christianity* (Jerusalem, 1988, 1992), pp. 108, 70.

[15] Stern, *Manifesto*, pp. 14–15.

[16] Ibid., p. 13.

Chapter 5

[17] Rabbi Benjamin Blech, *Understanding Judaism* (Northvale, 1991), p. xviii.

[18] Stern, pp. 125–126.

Chapter 6

[19] Harvey Lutzke, *The Book of Jewish Customs* (Northvale, 1986), p. 175.

[20] Rabbi Pinchas Kehati, *Mishnah: Seder Nezikin vol 4* (Jerusalem, 1994), VII 7.

[21] Rabbi Simcha Cohen, "Divine Origin of the Oral Torah," in *Return to the Source: Selected Articles on Judaism and Teshuva* (Jerusalem, 1984), p. 163.

[22] Ibid., p. 162.

[23] Ibid., p. 163.

[24] Ibid., p. 163.

[25] Ibid., p. 162.

[26] Ibid., pp. 168–169.

[27] David Flusser, *Jewish Sources in Early Christianity* (Tel Aviv, 1989), p. 21.

[28] Ibid., p. 22.

[29] See Mark 7:1–15 for an example (particularly verses 11–13).

[30] David Friedman, "The Positive Value of Rabbinic Literature," *Tishrei* vol. 2 no. 2 (Winter 1993–1994), 7–8.

[31] Ibid., p. 8.

[32] Kehati, VII 7.

[33] Contrast our interpretation of Deuteronomy 30:11–14 with the standard rabbinic usage of the passage. The typical rabbinic understanding is reflected in Rabbi Eliezar Berkovitz's classic treatise on halacha entitled *Not in Heaven*. Here he asserts that God delegated to those so qualified the task of defining halacha, the everyday practice of oral and written Torah. He says that we are not to look to "heaven," i.e., God, for halachic decisions, but rather to the oral tradition and decisions of the rabbis.

[34] E. William Bean, New Treasures, p. 80, quoting Pinchas Lapid.

[35] Ibid., p. 80 .

Chapter 7

[36] Merrill C. Tenney, *New Testament Introduction* (Leicester, 1961, 1988), p. 234.

[37] David H. Stern, *Jewish New Testament Commentary* (Jerusalem, 1993), p. 301.

[38] Hugh J. Schonfield, *The History of Jewish Christianity* (London), p. 54.

Please note that Schonfield experienced a major change in his life. Earlier in his career, he was a professing believer in Yeshua. That is when he wrote his *History*. However, things changed so drastically that he later wrote such heretical books as *The Passover Plot*. (See Daniel Juster, *Jewish Roots*, pp. 150–151.)

[39] The "blessing" is presently Blessing #12 of the Amidah and reads, "As for slanderers let there be no hope, and may all wickedness perish in an instant; and may all Your enemies be cut down speedily. May You speedily uproot, smash, cast down, and humble the wanton sinners—speedily in our days. Blessed are You, O Lord, who breaks and humbles wanton sinners." As you can see, the statements are much too broad to be exclusively against Messianic Jews. But the blessing would certainly have included them in its first inception into the Amidah.

[40] Samuele Bacchiocchi, *From Sabbath to Sunday* (Rome, 1977), p. 230

[41] Earle E. Cairns, *Christianity Through the Centuries* (Grand Rapids, 1954, 1973), p. 152.

[42] Edward J. Flannery, *The Anguish of the Jews* (Mahwah, 1985), pp. 50–52.

[43] "Law," *The Dictionary of New Testament Theology*, 1967, 1976, II 439–440.

[44] C. E. B. Cranfield, *Romans* (Edinburgh, 1975, 1990), II 853:

[45] "Law," *Dictionary*, II 445.

[46] Stern, *Commentary*, p. 395.

Notes

Notes

Notes

Continued Study

To continue your studies in the Torah, *First Fruits of Zion* offers many materials to assist you. We produce a bimonthly magazine from Jerusalem with many articles and teachings to encourage and educate those searching for the Jewish roots of their faith. We are also producing a study program entitled the *Torah Club,* which provides audio and written commentaries for each weekly Torah portion. These commentaries are designed to sharpen, educate and challenge students of the Word with the wonderful insights found in the Torah.

First Fruits of Zion
——————MAGAZINE——————
"A Promise of What is to Come"

A bimonthly magazine with Torah commentaries, news, testimonies and teaching on the Jewish roots of your faith. Written and produced in Jerusalem.

US and Israel: $27.00/year
All other countries: $38.00/year

Torah Club Volume I
Torah Treasures

"All Scripture is given by the inspiration of God, and is profitable for doctrine, for reproof, for correction, for instruction in righteousness, that the man of God may be complete..."
II Timothy 3:16-17

Our most popular edition of the Torah Club to date will take you through the entire Torah, introducing you to the world of Jewish thought through the anointing and inspiration of our talented Torah teachers. Volume I lays important foundations needed to fully enjoy and understand Volume II.

Torah Club Volume II
Yeshua in the Torah

"...all things must be fulfilled which were written in the Torah and the Prophets, and the Psalms concerning Me." Luke 24:44

Yeshua stated that every word written in the Torah pointed toward and spoke of Him. Volume II examines the Torah with this challenge in mind. How is Yeshua pictured in each portion? Ariel Berkowitz takes a revealing look at the way Messiah's love, grace and redemption are intertwined in every passage.

"I shed many a tear over the neglect of Torah in my life when we got our first parasha in May 1995. I was taught the Torah was a harsh bunch of do's and don'ts, and that the God of the Old Testament was a God of judgment. I found, instead, a loving God, beautiful promises, and teachings for my good. Now I cry for the beautiful nuggets found in each lesson."

The Lord bless you all, Bill and Sandy D.

As a member of the Torah Club, you will receive:

- One forty-five-minute audiocassette teaching for each Torah portion and Holy Day throughout the entire year. The teachings are in a discussion format between two of the leading Messianic rabbis in Israel.

- Extensive written teachings, notes and study questions on the Torah portions by Ariel Berkowitz.

- Full color binders for both your written and audio teachings.

- A subscription to *First Fruits of Zion* magazine

- 10% discount off all products listed in the *First Fruits of Zion* magazine product guide.

- *First Fruits of Zion* is a non-profit ministry. You can receive a tax credit of $25.00 per month for your participation in the Torah Club.

Membership dues: $35.00/month

For more information please contact: First Fruits of Zion, PO Box 620099 Littleton, CO 80162-0099, Phone (800) 775-4807 (303) 933-2119 Fax (303) 933-0997, E–mail ffoz@net-mgmt.com